T0028859

Advance Praise
Raising Conservative Kids in a Woke City

"You won't find clearer, more compelling, or more comforting wisdom than what Faust and Manning offer here. If you're a parent wondering how to raise strong, smart kids in a world gone mad, this book is for you. You'll finish Raising Conservative Kids feeling empowered to tackle the obstacles ahead!"

—Allie Beth Stuckey, Host of *Relatable*

"Stacy Manning and Katy Faust have written the indispensable guide for all parents who want to raise conservative children but don't have the benefit of living in a utopian commune on another planet sealed off from Planet Earth. Raising such kids involves neither sheltering them from the world, nor overexposing them to its toxins. It requires a deliberate method of inoculation, in which parents arm their kids with the resistant antibodies they will need to survive in—and even engage--our crazy world. This crisply written book lays this out clearly and concisely."

—Jay Richards, Heritage Foundation

"Successful authors often give new writers one piece of advice: 'write about what you know.' In Raising Conservative Kids in a WOKE City, Katy and Stacy don't imagine how to do it, they tell us what worked. As a fan of their style, intelligence and humor, I already knew the writing would be a joy to read. More importantly, as an admirer of their families, I attest to the truth of what God helped them achieve with their kids. There's another saying: 'information is power.' That's a lie. Until it's used, it's potential power. Put the power of this information to good use."

—Todd Herman, Host of
the *Todd Herman Show*

Also by Stacy Manning and Katy Faust

Them Before Us: Why We Need a
Global Children's Rights Movement

RAISING CONSERVATIVE KIDS IN A WOKE CITY

RAISING CONSERVATIVE KIDS IN A WOKE CITY

TEACHING HISTORICAL, ECONOMIC, AND BIOLOGICAL TRUTH IN A WORLD OF LIES

STACY MANNING & KATY FAUST

POST HILL
PRESS

A POST HILL PRESS BOOK
ISBN: 979-8-88845-006-2
ISBN (eBook): 979-8-88845-007-9

Raising Conservative Kids in a Woke City:
Teaching Historical, Economic, and Biological Truth in a World of Lies
© 2023 by Stacy Manning & Katy Faust
All Rights Reserved

Cover design by Cody Corcoran

No part of this book may be reproduced, stored in a retrieval system, or transmitted by any means without the written permission of the author and publisher.

Post Hill Press
New York • Nashville
posthillpress.com

Published in the United States of America
3 4 5 6 7 8 9 10

This book is dedicated to the parents who seek to join us as we walk the long road of raising conservative kids in a hostile culture.

TABLE OF CONTENTS

FOREWORD

by Yoram Hazony

Not long ago, American schools, universities, and media were overwhelmingly liberal. They consciously sought to inculcate liberal ideas such as free speech, freedom of religion, and academic freedom. As a part of this, they were willing to allow a certain space for the development of genuinely conservative points of view.

I grew up in a conservative home. As a kid I was usually expressing opinions on politics, religion, and much else that I had learned from my father, who was a proud Jew and staunchly conservative in his outlook. I attended liberal schools and universities in New Jersey. But in those days—in the 1970s and 1980s—my liberal teachers and professors really did allow me to express my views freely. They really did let me feel that my point of view was a legitimate part of the discussion, even though my conservative ideas were always a minority view.

But schools and universities aren't necessarily like that anymore. Neither are the movies our children watch or the news programs they are exposed to. Since the great cultural upheavals of 2020, Woke neo-Marxists have been actively calling the shots in thousands of formerly liberal institutions across America and in other democratic countries.

This means that millions of parents are now trying to raise their children in an environment that is no longer tolerant of the ideas and practices they are teaching in their conservative Christian or Jewish homes. A great many schools, universities, and media are now aggressively trying to make sure that children are being shaped in light of a revolutionary set of ideas on subjects such as sex, race, history, religion, the environment, and more.

How do you raise children when they are effectively under siege?

I have to admit that when Katy Faust told me that she and coauthor Stacy Manning were going to publish *Raising Conservative Kids in a Woke City*, I was skeptical. Children do best when they are raised in a community that shares their parents' values on fundamental issues. If the teachers at school are constantly, explicitly at odds with the parents' views on a range of crucial topics, it's time for mom and dad to find a better place for their kids to learn—whether this means relocating to a healthier community, joining with other parents to start a new school, or schooling your children at home.

But Katy is one of the most stubborn and persuasive personalities I have ever known. Her public speeches across America have become a major force that's changing the game for conservative parents across the United States. Her last book, *Them Before Us: Why We Need a Global Children's Rights Movement*, turned the tables on contemporary theories of the family, in which children have become a commodity that is used to allow adults to assert their rights. Using the language of children's rights, Katy has made an astonishingly compelling case for the traditional family. As she put it at a conference last year:

> A child is not an item to be cut and pasted into any adult relationship.... Respecting her rights means that all adults—single, married, gay, straight, fertile and infertile—have to do hard things on her behalf. Because the only alternative is to insist that she must do hard things for them. And that's an injustice.

In their new book, Katy and Stacy have done what I thought was impossible: they have produced a commonsense guide for parents who have suddenly found themselves sending their children out into hostile schools and a hostile community every single day.

At the heart of this book is the belief that parents in communities overrun by the present cultural revolution have no choice but to go to war for their children. This means engaging one's own children first on issues that we'd prefer that they not hear about until they are older. It means teaching them how to respond to Woke indoctrination and ensuring that they can hold their own against a predatory culture that seeks to turn them against what they have learned in their parents' homes.

A crucial insight in *Raising Conservative Kids in a Woke City* is the recognition that even in the middle of a city in the throes of cultural revolution, children have to have at least a small community of conservative adults around them. In addition to their parents, Stacy and Katy estimate that children need three or four more adults—grandparents, aunts and uncles, or adult neighbors—who are not a part of the revolution but actively teaching against it.

This means that conservatives, if they are to succeed at raising strong conservative children, have to set aside the old concept of a family as consisting of just two parents and their kids. Parents are the child's most important role models and their first line of defense. But parents just aren't enough. Children can't always be on perfect terms with their parents. They need other adults, family and nonfamily, to whom they can turn.

Stacy and Katy's *Raising Conservative Kids in a Woke City* is a gift, a blessing, and a lifeline to families under siege. Parents should read the book, watch these remarkable women speak on video, and bring them to their communities to teach.

Like the Jewish midwives in Egypt, Stacy and Katy have risked Pharoah's wrath to help us save our children.

Yoram Hazony
Author of *Conservatism: A Rediscovery*
January 31, 2023

INTRODUCTION

*S*tacy here.

My Consolation Prize, that is, my daughter Evelyn, is a one-woman pro-life rally. By consolation prize, I don't mean the whomp-whomp-whomp Price Is Right–type prizes. The one and only Manning girl-child is dazzling, and her exceptionalism consoles me as I watch her unfurl into womanhood so gracefully. She's proof of my outstanding parenting.[1]

Little fictions, like what a top-notch parent I am aside, we've done one thing right with each of our three kids: we got to them first. We've trained them with the cultural long road in mind. We've equipped them to fight the raging ideological war because if we have any chance of saving this country, the younger generations are going to have to pull their weight. Too many of Evelyn's peers have not been so well trained; their parents have not been first on the scene to impart the "why's" of their political worldview.

The failure of these parents to train their children provided Evelyn the opportunity to convert SIX of her friends from pro-choice to pro-life on a twenty-minute school bus ride during the sixth

---

[1] This little fiction of mine helps me endure her two brothers' seemingly endless horrible teacher conferences. She's my Consolation Prize that God saw fit to sandwich between Dynamite and his older brother, Bumpy Ride.

grade. In SIX separate instances, she arrived home with another successful conversion to report. Her story was the same every time. Well, it wasn't the same from Evelyn's perspective every time; the first time she decided to push back and make her pro-life case, she was awfully nervous. We live in a deep blue city in a dark blue state, and you can be nearly certain that you're talking to someone on the left every time you open your mouth in these parts.

Evelyn is so passionately pro-life, and her horror at the practice is so visceral, that she tears up when she talks about the evils of abortion. She has also been armed with facts, she's confident in her beliefs, and she has the luxury of knowing she's right. Her first successful conversion was such a victory for her, she breathlessly briefed me on all the juicy details after school that day, marveling that her friend "didn't know why she thought what she thought about abortion." Every conversion that followed only emboldened her. In every instance these kids thought they knew what they didn't and her conversations with them unfolded the same way each time. When she presented them with truth and statistics? They changed their eleven-year-old minds about murdering babies in the womb on a twenty-minute bus ride.

. . .

That's what intentional conservative parenting looks like in America circa century twenty-one.

Not so long ago when the "United" part of The United States was still mostly true, the American people's vibe was generally "down with Socialism," we knew that men who played dress-up and wore lady-face could never actually become women, and we mostly agreed that polygamy was regressive and harmed women and children. But, while we weren't looking, in short order, the world went mad. Even if you weren't raised in a religious or conservative household, you can see the madness. It's quite obvious that things just ain't right because unlike today, you had the luxury of growing up in a country still tethered to reality.

In one short decade parents of all stripes—Christians, conservatives, and middle-of-the-road types—have looked up to find themselves parenting in the Upside Down, doing a job fraught with more difficulty than munching on a big bowl of broken glass. What happened?

WOKE happened.

Wikipedia identifies Woke as an adjective meaning "alert to racial prejudice and discrimination." If that is what being Woke was limited to, Wokists[2] would be happily at home among conservatives, as we right-wing types don't cotton to injustice and we're all about championing individual rights; further, prejudice and discrimination is about as un-American as it gets. But because like nearly every institution in the United States, Wikipedia has a massive left-wing bias, it failed to wholly capture Woke.[3] Wokists hold a culturally hegemonic worldview that views every subject, institution, Netflix series, and human interaction through the lens of group identity, and

---

[2]   Throughout this book, we will refer to those who zealously promote a Woke worldview as "Wokists." But not everyone on the left is Woke. Many liberals are also uncomfortable with how Wokists are consuming our institutions but are unsure how to stop it and are going along for the sake of survival.

[3]   Elon Musk defines Woke this way: "At its heart, wokeness is divisive, exclusionary, and hateful. It basically gives mean people a shield to be cruel, armored in false virtue."

then uses every weapon at its disposal to pit one group against the other under the guise of social justice.

On paper, Woke sounds noble—as is the case with most leftist causes—but the real-life outcome of the Wokist worldview is the rending of our social fabric. You know you're in the Woke's presence when emotion instead of facts are the basis for their opinions and its dissenters are labeled "such-and-such-phobes"; when they assume hatred of women, gays, immigrants, minorities, trans, and so on is the motive for disagreements about complex issues, and not conforming to their increasingly extreme policy goals is because you want people to *die*.[4] Wokists have laid claim to nearly every board room, school, and Thanksgiving dinner conversation. They've captured our institutions—entertainment, academia, medicine, education, and the entire Democrat Party. Woke mandates that every knee bow and every tongue confess its truth, and if you refuse to submit, the "love and tolerance" mob will impose serious personal and professional consequences.

You're reading this book because you *know* that the Wokists are a pestilence, devouring everything in their path; they're consuming our country, our workplaces, and especially our children. The gut instinct of any decent parent is to shelter your kids; being fairly decent-ish parents ourselves we can relate. Except shelter is temporary, the Woke swarm is massive, and our crop of young people are their favorite resource to consume. You must teach your children what the swarm looks like, how to identify it, and *how and what to think when*

---

[4] Get the shot or you will kill my grandma! Or if you won't allow your child to be sexually mutilated, they're going to commit suicide.

the Wokists descend on them. You must equip your kids to survive the Woke plague and how to emerge from it unscathed. You want them to be able to answer difficult questions, but you also don't want to destroy their innocence. What's today's sane, rational parent to do?[5]

Perhaps you're stuck, like we are, in a city dominated by Woke ideologues. A city where mainstream media, social media, your kids' teachers and peers, your neighbors, and maybe even your church folk have bought into the "progressive" insanity.

Are you doomed? And more importantly are your children doomed?

You bet you they are. Unless you become very intentional about worldview training from the moment your sweet little angel baby can form complete sentences. The bad news, overtaxed parent, is that this job cannot be outsourced. The good news is that you are exactly the right person for the job.

Before we get into the "how to's," a quick definition. When you hear the word "conservative," we imagine you think of big-military-loving, small government, flag-waving, low-tax-cheering, homeschooling, gun-nut, prepper, Jesus-Freak types. In other words, *our* kind of Americans. For the record, two decades ago this was mostly true, but these days, because the other side has gone certifiably bat sh*t crazy, *conservative* now defines anyone that recognizes historical, economic, and biological reality. If that's you, welcome to the party, you

---

5   Or even the nuttier ones for that matter.

right-wing nut. I hope you brought along a nice cold beverage to choke down that big red pill.

The late Andrew Breitbart was famous for saying, "Politics is downstream from culture," and our polity has become polluted because too many Americans are distracted by our sensualist, you-do-you, amoral culture. Many mistakenly believe that governmental dysfunction is for other people to fix, but if the rise of Woke has crystallized anything, it's that you may not be interested in politics, but politics are interested in you.[6]

So, fellow conservative, it's past time for you to engage—especially if you've been apathetic and tuned-out till now. The truth is, God almighty does exist and He ordains the times and boundaries of nations and people, even for you Godless pagans.[7] In other words, you are not living here and now by accident, and neither are your children. He put y'all here, today, for a reason. As our Jesus Freak friends would say, "You are to be *in* the world, but not *of* the world." For those of you who don't yet belong to Jesus's fan club, the Freaks understand this to mean that we are not to be *transformed by culture*, but be *transformers of culture*.

Speaking of Jesus Freaks, an introduction is in order.

Stacy Manning. Senior editor for Them Before Us, Stacy is a standard issue, stay-at-home suburban mom, author, and side-hustle professional. It's also widely accepted that Mrs. Manning is responsible for inventing the raised middle finger, a.k.a. the Bird of Freedom. She and her husband

---

[6]   Hat tip Shakespeare.
[7]   Speaking as formerly Godless pagans ourselves.

of twenty-something years[8] are raising their three children behind enemy lines in a suburb just outside Seattle. When she's not sticking her meddling fingers in another writer's work, she is barefoot in the kitchen making her husband a sammich.

Katy Faust. Formerly considered a peacemaking pastor's wife, Katy is founder and president of Them Before Us, a global children's rights nonprofit. Between soccer carpool and church duties, she's a mom on a mission against the progressive overreach, a globe-trotting speaker, hand-shaking policy influencer, and regular contributor to a variety of conservative outlets. Katy testifies and publishes widely on controversial topics such as "men and women are different" and "children should not be bought and sold." She helped design the JV edition of the Witherspoon Institute's CanaVox, which studies sex, gender, marriage, and relationships from a natural law perspective. She and her husband of twenty-five years are raising their four children on the outskirts of Seattle.

We are both still deep in mothering territory; between us we've got kids from elementary school to college, seven all told. Obviously, we would be much more comfortable publishing this book after successfully launching our broods, our mothering crowns adorned with seven shining examples of conservative adult children. But alas, the time for counting chickens prior to hatching is upon us and we've accepted the possibility that we might eat a lifetime of crow casserole should one of our kids become a Bernie Bro in post-production.

---

[8] A quarter freaking century. Unbelievable.

However, our country doesn't have the luxury of waiting to see if all seven Manning/Faust offspring embrace the free market prior to sharing these parenting principles with you. Evidenced by the fact that in every interaction—whether conversations with close friends or talking heads on major platforms—the same question arises: How can we keep the Wokists from consuming our kids? We needed this book yesteryear, and we regret not knowing how much.

In these chapters, we will share our hard-won wisdom on how to raise conservative kids deep in the trenches of one of America's most left-of-liberal bastions. We've also committed the sin of (cue the gasps of pearl clutching, judge-y Christian Homeschooling Moms) sending our kids through the dreaded public school system.[9] While we have been purposeful about finding our people, which is a huge support in terms of effective inculcation of values, we have not sheltered our children from the world. Rather, we have identified and implemented principles and processes that walk the line between protection and exposure, sheltering and equipping.

In this book, we are going to share tales of our kids totally killing it. They are an awesome bunch, and we're proud that they are holding fast to their convictions, but they're not perfect. With seven between us, we've got plenty of material to work with, and you'll have to suffer a number of mom brags. That said, we've certainly walked through some epic failures with each of them, but the choice to share those failures is theirs to make. Thus, we will keep exclusively to cheerleading[10]

---

[9]   Katy's kids have picked up a few years of private school here and there.
[10] Almost exclusively.

in this book. We are not perfect, and neither are our kids. So as you read, keep in mind that raising kids in general, and raising conservative kids in a hostile environment especially, is messy and wildly uncomfortable.

We are in this with you, conservative mom and dad. We too feel that everyone and everything is against us. Probably because it is. But we assure you, if you get on and stay on the job, you can successfully raise competent, conservative kids.

Our failed politicians have shown us that we cannot count on elections to rescue us from the Upside Down in which we currently find ourselves. We wholly believe the next generation is capable of righting America, and that it's the smallest governmental body, the family, that is the most powerful weapon against the Woke.

CHAPTER 1

←——————————————→

WHAT IS CONSERVATISM?

*S*tacy here.

My childhood was a Jerry Springer–style sh*t show. My father was a booze-fueled, race-car-driving womanizer. In other words, a bona fide yahoo. I'd say he had a difficult home life as a child, but the word "home" implies that his family had an address. While he and his three siblings surely enjoyed their waterfront view of the bayou, an address is not a thing when you're sleeping in a four-door sedan. My mother was provided a childhood that, from all outward appearances, should have culminated in a well-adjusted woman, but she's been a hot mess most of her life. My parents were a match for all the wrong, dysfunctional reasons, which made for a chaos-laden childhood. My mother was obsessed with my father and misapprehended that, by sheer will, she could transform him from yahoo into the kind of man he had no capacity to be. Her misguided pursuit caused her to sacrifice the physical safety and emotional security of my brother and me. In fact, I believe the regular visits the police paid to my childhood home to quell, yet another, liquor-fueled fiasco lie at the heart of the "thing" I have for men in uniform.

You might be thinking that such an exciting childhood sounds like a rockin' good time, but I must admit to feeling a tad slighted in the parent lottery.

It was a maximum drama, low-information environment, and my education was not high on the list of my parents' priorities. Therefore, getting the most out of my K–12 public school education was entirely my responsibility, and I approached it with the maturity of a child. To this undereducated, uninformed child's eyes, the liberals were the cool kids in the miasma of the seventies and eighties. Since liberal sounded an awful lot like liberty to me, and in my mind, liberty meant freedom, I was obviously one of the cool liberal kids.

Enter Rush Limbaugh and Dr. Laura. I began listening to their radio shows at around age eighteen. Up until this pivotal development, I'd viewed myself as a victim of my ridiculous parents, but Dr. Laura, catalyst of my mind's reformation, helped me realize that having been victimized by my parents, a victim I was not. That important differentiation gave me real power over my life, and Rush Limbaugh schooled me in the true nature of American politics.[1]

I realized that of all the things I instinctually believed—such as the importance of family, that markets should be free and trade unfettered, traditional values, love of country, and that the delightful and beautiful differences between men and women should be celebrated—none of these were liberal values. I was, in fact, a conservative. I am profoundly grateful for the impact these two straight-talking strangers had on my life as I came of age. I credit the influence of Rush and the Good Doctor for keeping me from

---

[1] His show—and the fact that I listened to it—drove my politically illiterate, tribally democrat mother nuts.

following in my yahoo family's tradition of drug addiction and teen pregnancy; they informed my ability to achieve escape velocity from the event horizon of my dysfunctional upbringing, and as a result, my husband and I have created a mostly drama-free marriage for my three children.

. . .

No matter your education or lack thereof, no matter your age, no matter your background, it's never too late to begin to see the world as it actually is and conduct yourself accordingly. In other words, it's never too late to change your mind and become a conservative.

We've titled this book *Raising Conservative Kids in a Woke City*. Not raising red-state kids, or libertarian kids, or Trumpian kids, or anti-Woke kids. Being a conservative is not just about rejecting the Wokist worldview, nor is it simply being *anti*-Left. This chapter is intended to explain exactly what you and your conservative kids should be *for*.

Foundationally, conservatism properly views our rights as bestowed upon us by God and that our government is established to protect those God-given rights. This is the most important distinction between progressivism and conservatism because, when you consider the opposite viewpoint, you quickly realize that a government responsible for conferring rights upon its citizenry possesses the power to revoke those rights. This fundamental, opposing perspective is at the heart of the deep divide in our nation. Today, a dangerously large portion of our citizenry views government as the grantor of rights, and that necessitates conservatives stand up and push back.

Conservative philosophy, at its core, recognizes and conforms to the base nature of human beings; that's why the conservative approach to problem solving seeks its solutions by considering historical facts, accounting for biological realities, and relies on observable, time-tested economic principles. Conservative ideology is sound and durable[2] because it respects the unchanging, often ugly, condition of mankind.

Conservatives are rightly appalled by the outlandish power grabs of our behemoth federal government, scandalized by the *New York Times* routine celebration of consensual non-monogamy, and alarmed by child-grooming masquerading as sex-ed curriculum. But being conservative doesn't mean you reject unconstitutional acts and moral decay just for the sake of rejection. Being a conservative means opposing an ever-expanding administrative state *because* history illustrates that federalism is superior to authoritarianism; it means defending the nature of the traditional family *because* we know it gives children the greatest chance of successfully launching into adulthood; it means rejecting leftist, government-centered school policy *because* we believe parents are foremost responsible for steering their children's education. Being a conservative requires you to understand what you are *for*.

Old, time-tested ideas are generally the best ideas. New, so-called progressive ideas are often *regressive* in practice

---

[2]   The only constant of the progressive goal posts is that they are never stationary. They've moved so far that noteworthy liberals, the likes of Bari Weiss, Bill Maher, and Dave Rubin for example, have been pushed out of the mainstream left for failing to champion the Woke bona fides required to remain in the ranks.

because they eschew the nature of man. Such ideas include swapping police for social workers, or that the "means of production" are better controlled by the government than the free-market, or pushing the belief that men and women can be "nonbinary." Such notions are cute when bandied about during late-night college dorm room debates, but in practice, these beliefs result in human suffering and death. Good ideas, very few of which have emerged in the recent past, must be conserved.

So, what exactly do we mean by *conservative*?

You've picked up a book by two moms who hold a total of zero advanced degrees, and we've no delusions of political scholars' grandeur. So, if you're looking for a meaty exploration of conservatism, we'd recommend *Conservatism: A Rediscovery* by Yoram Hazony. However, while we might not have expensive honorifics behind our names, you needn't be a scholar to observe that this country's dysfunction runs deep. Therefore, because we are patriotic Americans who want our grandchildren to inherit a freer, morally healthy country, we've taken our best shot at outlining what must be conserved for the sake of America's future.[3]

Conservatism requires conservation, and our aim is to help you train your children to conserve and forward the best historical, biological, economic, and governmental ideas. As noted, principles that promote human flourishing are often derived from ancient concepts, whether informed by nature or observed by the great philosophers of antiquity. Integrating

---

[3] You'll find there's a lot of room under the conservative tent to mingle among the Ronald Reagan fan club and the "AUDIT THE FED!!" crowd.

ancient truths with natural law enabled our founders to draft the most durable constitution ever written. And while most of these time-tested principles have endured through the centuries, many of these proven concepts are facing distinct and unprecedented challenges. The following principles are those we believe are the most at risk and therefore the most important to conserve in the minds of our children.

On the nature of America. Conservatives seek to *conserve* the integrity of the nation-state. We believe that national identity, national borders, national sovereignty, and national pride are *good*.[4] We reject the notion of a "global citizenry" and repudiate bureaucratic interference from international bodies such as the United Nations.[5]

Conservatives also seek to conserve the founding principles of *this* nation—limited government, separation of powers, checks and balances, federalism, republicanism,[6] and individual rights. These principles align with human nature and thus have enabled the United States to become the most prosperous society the world has ever known. John Adams rightly observed that "our Constitution was made only for a moral and religious people. It is wholly inadequate to the government of any other." The success of America's revolutionary design for limited government is dependent on whether we launch virtuous, self-governing children into adulthood. More succinctly,

---

4   Not just the nation of America, but the goodness of nationhood in general. It's good for Poles to prioritize Poland, for Indians to believe that India is the greatest nation, and for Brits to reclaim national power from the European Union.
5   Some of the worst violators of human rights—Saudi Arabia, Pakistan, China, Cuba, and Russia—have occupied prominent positions on the UN Human Rights Council. You don't want the UN anywhere near your daily life.
6   Small r republicanism. Look it up.

as Chuck Colson[7] often said, "It's the conscience or the constable." In lesser words,[8] our children *will* be governed—the question is, will they be self-governed adults because they've been raised to hold morally informed convictions, or will they be governed by a tyrannical nanny state?

Conservatives venerate the truth of our country's history, both by recognizing the noble sacrifices previous generations made to form and keep our nation free, and by acknowledging the ways America has fallen short, such as withholding the rights of minorities and women.[9]

Religion/freedom of conscience. Not freedom *from* religion, but freedom *of* religion. Separation of church and state was conceived not to protect the government from religious beliefs but vice versa. Conservatives seek to preserve the right to practice our faith and live out our convictions, especially in the public square. The right to free religious expression is inextricable from our God-given right to liberty.

Many people mistakenly believe that religion is biased and secularism is neutral, but a cursory examination of Wokist

---

[7] Founder of the Colson Center, conservative Christian superstar.

[8] Read: our words.

[9] Judging America by its failures rather than by its founding principles is akin to obtaining the best cookie recipe of all time, substituting butter with I Can't Believe It's Not Butter, swapping all-purpose for cassava flour, and then declaring that the recipe, and not your execution of it, was flawed.

cult behavior illustrates that these radicals can be the most dogmatic of all religious congregations in America. The Woke keep their own liturgical calendar replete with holy days and a month-long celebration of PRIDE,[10] they've instituted their own religious lexicon,[11] they ordain an intersectional hierarchy of priests,[12] they excommunicate[13] members who defy their official yet ever-changing dogma,[14] and their army of leftist evangelists posing as educators proselytize in nearly every public school.

On the nature of man and woman. We seek to conserve the reality that men and women are gloriously distinct and both make equally important contributions to society. We stand firm on the truth that those complementary differences profoundly impact human survival and flourishing.

Because men and women are, down to their very DNA, biologically different, men can never become women, nor vice versa. Thus, men, women, boys, and girls should be encouraged to appreciate and embrace their physical bodies because irreversible damage[15] is done when human beings

---

[10] Formerly known as one of the seven deadly sins. Just sayin'.

[11] New-fangled words like cis, Latinx, and gender affirming care, intended to identify the speaker as one of the "enlightened."

[12] Ibram X. Kendi, "anti-racist" racism hustler, will absolve your workplace of white guilt for a mere ten grand per speech.

[13] Cancel.

[14] "Progressive revelation" at its finest.

[15] Abigail Shrier's book *Irreversible Damage: The Transgender Craze Seducing Our Daughters* is a must-read if you want to be wildly depressed and wickedly informed about the damage gender ideology is doing to our children.

are chemically and surgically altered to conform to a gender-confused mind.

Because sex differences are real and consequential, uncompromising biological separation of men's and women's sports is essential; and distinct divisions should be enforced in locker rooms, bathrooms, and changing rooms.

On the nature of marriage. Marriage, as defined prior to 2015[16] is not equivalent to gay marriage. Singularly, the union of man and woman create the next generation, and a child has a right to be raised by the two people responsible for his or her existence. Good government policy incentivizes the union of a child's parents for life. The right of children to be known and loved by both their mother and father is such an important concept that we've already published a deep dive into the subject titled *Them Before Us: Why We Need a Global Children's Rights Movement*. Shameless plugs aside, it's worth a read.[17]

On the nature of the parent-child relationship. Just as children have a right to their own parents, parents have a right to their children. Those rights have corresponding obligations and duties such as protecting, providing, caring for, and educating children. Statistically, a child's parents are the most

---

[16] Before the Supreme Court swerved out of their constitutional lane and legislated marriage law from the bench.

[17] It's a pretty solid effort, and we could use more sales. Please and thank you.

connected to, protective of, and invested in their children,[18] thus parents have the right to direct their children's upbringing and to make medical decisions on their behalf, inclusive of whether to vaccinate and especially sexual health guidance. Parental authority is paramount in school choice, curriculum selection, and in all matters of gender identity and sex education in public school. Children belong to their parents, not to the state, not to doctors, and certainly not to schools.

On the right to life. Every human being inherently possesses the right to life from the moment of conception until natural death, thus we seek to conserve the scientifically undeniable position that a child in the womb is a human being with rights deserving protection. We are also passionately pro-choice in that we ardently endorse *choosing wisely* when engaging in baby-making activity.[19] Following conception, the adults responsible for sexy time are obligated to protect both their child's right to life and their child's right to their mother and father. Should an adult be unable or unwilling to protect and provide for their child, a just society doesn't kill babies; it adopts them.

On the matter of race. People of all races are created in the image of God and the dignity of the individual should

---

[18]   *Them Before Us*, chapter 2. Really. It will change your life.
[19]   Sex.

be center-stage politically, culturally, and interpersonally. Conservatives believe that merit should be the sole consideration when assessing a person's potential. We believe it is immoral to afford privilege or deny opportunity because of the color of someone's skin. Conservatives believe true diversity is realized only by a diversity of ideas, and that using skin color as a measure of diversity is pedestrian and insulting. It is racist to deny *or* select someone for employment or enrollment in higher education based on race, and such policies should be rejected outright, in all forms, in every way.

"Anti-racism" measures, such as decreasing academic standards for minorities or implementing affirmative action quotas, harm those they intend to help; such policies foster a mismatch between students and institutions that disproportionately diminishes academic success for minorities, reinforces racial stigmas, and seeds self-doubt.[20] It is immoral for society to sow distrust between its citizens by requiring less or more of one subset of humans than another. True racial progress is measured not in *equity*[21] but in *equality* of opportunity.

On economics. Controlling the means of production[22] is often a predicate for crimes against humanity. The worst regimes on earth, those that have racked up the highest death toll, have all

---

[20] Richard Sander and Stuart Taylor Jr., "The Painful Truth about Affirmative Action: Why Racial Preferences in College Admissions Hurt Minority Students— and Shroud the Education System in Dishonesty," *The Atlantic*, October 2, 2012.

[21] Woke-speak for equal outcomes.

[22] This is the essence of socialism; it's about top-down economic control, not hippie BS, "Hey man, can't we just share?" pacifism.

exercised some level of market control to achieve their dictatorial ambitions. Mankind's inherent dignity cannot be fully realized unless people are afforded the exercise of free choice that only voluntary labor and trade can provide. The free market is the most moral means of commerce.

Progressives arrogantly profess that the failed attempts to create a thriving communist/socialist state were the result of bad execution, not the inescapable outcome of bad ideas. In their hubris, the "real socialism has never really been tried" crowd maintain that those who've gone before us simply weren't as sophisticated as we modern folk; that if the *right* people were in charge, a socialist utopia would finally be realized. Therefore, in the face of those that refuse to learn from history, conservatism requires constant vigilance against the ever-present threat of collectivism and the danger it poses to the American way of life.

We imagine[23] more than a few of you were thinking, "duh" as you read through our list because *you know what you believe.* What wakes you at the witching hour is *how* to successfully inculcate your kids with your beliefs when every institution—school, media, and maybe even your extended family—seems bent on dismantling them. So, if you're with us, you've got two choices: either lie down and die[24] or fight like hell and train your kids for the battle.

It's also possible, darling reader, that you have been playing the part of The Problem in our country. Perhaps your stomach is churning as you consider the numerous times

---

[23] Hope, really.
[24] You lie-down-and-die folks? Get off our lawn.

you've voted against America's best interest at the ballot box. If we've accurately assessed the state of your digestive tract, the most powerful way to start the journey into right thinking, and rescue your children from this toxic culture, is to come clean about your misguided progressive ways. Honesty with yourself, and confession to your kids, is a powerful way to escape the Woke cult and begin actively pushing back against the Wokist worldview *as a team*.

America is in decline because American parents have raised too many *children*, childish adults who cry for "safe spaces" when they are presented with ideas they are *against*. As parents we must approach parenting with the mindset of raising *adults* capable of defending what they are *for*.

No matter where your ideological odyssey begins, it's a journey you are capable of traveling. You *can* do it because you *have* to do it. No one is coming to rescue us freedom-loving, free-speaking, free-thinking Americans from this cultural war, and for our kids' sake, boots-on-the-ground time is upon us.

CHAPTER 2

←——————————→

TRAINING REQUIRES GETTING TO YOUR KID FIRST

Rescuing your kids from the scourge of Woke ideology is a dilemma especially pressing for the 90 percent of American parents who send their kids to public school. Every day your kids are exposed to the dominant Wokist culture that tells them abortion is simply a "choice" and that Big Pharma, with a plastic surgeon assist, can transform a boy into a girl. You wonder if today is the day your kids' blue-haired teacher goes viral for filming theyself[1] teaching their class of crumb-crunchers to pledge allegiance to the gay pride flag,[2] or if they'll come home and ask you to explain why white-skinned people are guilty of possessing the "spirit murdering of Black and Brown children."[3]

Black Lives Matter's "queer affirming" curriculum has infiltrated our schools under the guise of anti-racist

---

[1]   When we're not mocking preferred pronouns, we're refusing to use them.
[2]   Yes. This actually happened.
[3]   Ya. This did too.

instruction, and your kids can even purchase their very own Team BLM jersey from the main office at their middle school. Our school district no longer requires teachers to conference with parents; instead we are made to suffer inane "student led conferences" while the PRIDE-pin-adorned[4] advisory teacher loiters nearby, in a classroom littered with leftist, anti-capitalism propaganda, located at the end of a hallway covered with "hate has no home here"[5] and "silence is violence" posters. We public school parents have no illusions that our nation's classrooms have been overrun by Wokist acolytes.

"Get your kids out of the public schools!" is the shame-inducing go-to solution repeated, ad nauseum, by our well-meaning conservative brethren. Of course, if it's possible for one parent to take on your children's education full-time, DO IT. But for many, that's not an option. Fleeing to red states is another popular solution that an alarming number of conservatives are choosing. We salute those who have fled, and we envy the right-sized housing prices you're cashing in on. But for the many of us whose responsibilities dictate our zip codes—whether because of an ailing parent, a business that can't be moved to South Dakota, or a child custody arrangement—a more attainable solution is required.

---

[4]   The flair on this one would get an A+ from the restaurant manager in *Office Space*.

[5]   Spoiler. Hate has a happy home wherever you see a slogan stating otherwise. It's just the *right* kind of hate.

Parenting Is about Training

Parents are understandably desperate to avoid conversations about the meaning of "pansexual," and many would rather lock their kids in the basement till they're thirty before they had to describe what a phalloplasty[6] is to their twelve-year-old. We can relate to your desperation and agree that basement-dwelling would be a great strategy; that is, if the goal of parenting was to keep your kids safe. But it's not. Parenting is training, and in a Woke city, training starts early.

The most glaring example of the negative outcome that results when safety is mistakenly prioritized above all else was the government response to COVID-19. According to our elites, safety was the singular aim once the virus leaked out of that Wuhan lab, and overnight "stay safe!"[7] became the maxim chirped ad nauseam by store clerks everywhere.[8] "Safety" came at the high cost of two years of childhood education, socialization, employment, and mental health. Forced isolation pushed suicides to record numbers, and deaths of despair from drug and alcohol use skyrocketed. Academic achievement, especially among at-risk and minority students, may never recover from the teachers' unions'[9] demands to keep themselves *safe*. When it comes to nuclear war, safety is an appropriate goal. When it comes to human maturation and thriving, safety at any cost is the enemy.

---

[6] Surgically stripping skin from a girl's forearm to create a faux penis. "Gender-affirming care" is legal butchery.

[7] Who knew there could be a more detestable salutation than "welcome in."

[8] Only the "essential" workers, you know, the ones at the weed shop and the abortion clinics.

[9] In the running for Most Corrupt Institution in modern life.

The devastation caused by the government's pandemic response is a wide-scale lesson in the dangers of making safety priority number one. On a smaller scale, modern parenting has demonstrated that a safety-first mentality results in unprepared, emotionally immature adults.[10]

Parents who elevate safety über alles[11] are hampering our country's future. They're unleashing young adults who become unhinged upon hearing the phrase "All Lives Matter" and need trigger warnings before reading Shakespeare. It's a terrible approach for any parent, but it's especially dangerous if you intend to raise kids who can overcome the Woke world.

• • •

Katy here.

Before we had kids, my husband and I were steeped in youth ministry. During these years we observed two parenting styles, generally polar opposites of one another. One was a safety-first cocooning, which shrouded kids in protection. These kids weren't allowed to listen to secular music or read Harry Potter, *and they entered college[12] having never heard an origin story other than six-day creation. They spent their formative years totally sheltered from different worldviews. These were the kids whose faith could be undone by one viewing of* The Da Vinci Code.

---

[10] In fact, American parents are so consumed by the safety-above-all mentality that, ridiculously, booster seats for middle schoolers are required by law in some states. Like here, where Katy and I break the law every day.

[11] German lingo dog-whistle for those who believe anyone to their political right is a Nazi.

[12] The freshman fifteen was a given for these kids.

On the other side of the spectrum were the hey-whatever-man[13] parents. These types offered no guidance on entertainment choices and allowed unrestricted access to screens.[14] In essence, overexposure to the world with few, if any, boundaries. These kids were often out of control as teens, having never been taught self-governance or made to suffer the consequences of their bad choices. When their kids' antics became overly dangerous or embarrassing, these foolhardy parents would try in vain to rein in their middle and high schoolers. Except they had missed the basic training window,[15] and because they never forced their preschooler to face the music for shoplifting a pack of gum, they were dealing with a high schooler arrested for shoplifting at Abercrombie.

We concluded that when we had children, the best parenting strategy would be to do what we could to emphasize maximum boundaries, consequences, and discipline for our young children, and then gradually lean out, so by the time high school was upon us, our kids would largely be self-managing.[16] We wanted them to encounter every challenge to their faith, morals, and worldview while they were still under our roof, so we would be there to evaluate conflicting ideas with them. Our goal wasn't primarily to keep them safe—either physically or ideologically. We knew we couldn't make the world safe for our kids; so our goal was to prepare them to stand on their own, and that meant age-appropriate exposure and risk.

In his book *Wild at Heart*,[17] author John Eldredge describes the creation story in Genesis in a beautiful and very accurate

---

[13] Much like Stacy's yahoo parents, but these parents added a dose of church.
[14] Today's version lets their kid pick their gender. Were we in charge, parenting privileges would be revoked.
[15] Don't be that parent—read chapter 6.
[16] Heavily influenced by *Parenting with Love and Logic.*
[17] Must-read on manhood and raising sons.

way. He observes that while God is busy creating creation—making lions, tigers, and bears, all killers of men—God does not assess His creation as *safe*, but rather Eldredge notes that "God saw that it was *good*."[18] This world is not a "safe" place, and it's not intended to be; your body, mind, and ego will, and should, be challenged. Safety-first does not make for a life that teaches or challenges one to make better choices or learn new things. After all, what is the point of this life?[19] Staying "safe" at home, no friends, no work, no socializing? Been there, done that, not great. Life is to be lived, in all its messiness, and it is *good*.

Your goal as parents, especially conservative parents living in America's leftist hellholes, is not to keep your child *safe*, shielded from the madness and insulated from the insanity. Your job is to *train* your kids to stand firm against the ceaseless assault on their principles, because they know what they are *for* and *why* they are for it.

That loooooong introduction was mostly written for moms. Mom is generally the parent most concerned with the immediate emotional well-being of their sweet babies.[20] We women tend to prepare the road for the child rather than prepare the child for the road. Therefore, fellow moms, you must fight your overprotectionist instincts and talk to your children about topics that make you squirm way before you're ready.

---

[18]   Direct quote, obvi.
[19]   "Get busy living or get busy dying"—Red, *The Shawshank Redemption*.
[20]   See chapter 3 of our first book, *Them Before Us: Why We Need a Global Children's Rights Movement*.

Get to Your Kids First

We live in the age of information and it is impossible to shield kids from ideas, both good and disastrous. This requires you to purposefully construct a right-thinking perspective through which children can assess the veracity of the conflicting messages and downright lies delivered firehose style daily. This means you're going to have to broach many subjects that you wish you didn't have to discuss with them earlier than you'd like. They're going to hear about porn and white privilege from someone; that someone needs to be you.

Of the challenges for modern parents, the internet ranks among the greatest. With one click kids can learn how a diesel engine works, and a second click can take them to the gay-men-having-sex-covered-in-diesel-fuel fetish site.[21] The problem is not that kids can't access information; it's that they have *too much* information, and often they have to discern which of the conflicting claims they've been presented with are true.

In an information age, it's not a matter of getting information; it's a question of which sources of information your kids will consider authoritative. And that's why YOU, conservative mom or dad, must establish yourself as *the* authority in your child's eyes. You want them to trust you, consult you, and rely on you for trustworthy answers. That will not happen unless you get to them first.

. . .

---

[21] Mr. Manning is in the automotive business. He was fifty-three years old when Google introduced him to the world of gay diesel sex fetishists. On his work computer, no less.

There's a strange phenomenon when it comes to learning; Hillary Morgan Ferrer[22] calls it the "founder's principle." This principle describes a dynamic we've both watched play out in our kids and their friend groups. The founder's principle asserts that whoever gets to kids first will, in their mind, automatically be considered the expert.

For example, say your son is entirely unaware of pornography and discovers it via a classmate's smart phone? That classmate just became his go-to porn expert. If your daughter hears the word "queer" for the first time from a YouTuber, we'd wager[23] she'll seek out that YouTuber when she wants more information about sexual identity. If history teacher by day/BLM acolyte by night Mx.[24] Bell is the first to introduce Jim Crow laws, who will your child consider the expert on racial matters? It won't be you.

Disabuse[25] yourself of the notion that if you don't introduce your kids to matters of abortion, slavery, homosexuality, and "equity," nobody will. In reality you're going to have to talk to your kids about sensitive topics and concepts much sooner than you would prefer. If you don't, their peers, the internet, and their teachers will happily fill that void for you, which means they'll have rights of first refusal for every follow-up conversation.

Getting to kids first means you must address every issue that runs afoul of conservative values. If you're not sure which

---

[22] Author of *Mama Bear Apologetics*. Once you're done with this book, go get that one.
[23] We don't wager on just anything; Katy's too cheap, and Stacy couldn't gamble her way out of a paper sack.
[24] There is just so much stupid, it's hard to manage. We know.
[25] Hat tip Ron DeSantis's overuse of that new vocabulary word.

issues to broach, imagine the conversations you would NOT want your child having with Bernie Sanders, AOC, or Kamala Harris and put those topics at the top of the list.

Smartphones—The Devil's Playground

You can kiss your chance of getting to your kids first goodbye if you've provided them a portal to hell.[26] Giving your young child unsupervised access to the internet is an excellent way to hand your authority to online strangers who will relish ushering them into a Wokist worldview or worse. As we explain in chapter 6, your primary job in elementary school is to saturate your child in truth and beauty[27] while filtering out damaging and destructive ideas. A smart phone is guaranteed to undermine both aims.

The usurpation of your authority and the threat to effective worldview training aren't the only reasons to say *no* when every other parent is saying *yes* to a phone.

Illicit content is one obvious reason to keep screens out of your child's life, but the more insidious problem with screens for the two-to-six-year-old crowd is that screens interfere with brain development. These are the years children learn to be industrious.[28] They are wired to create at this stage—building with blocks, configuring dinosaurs in a football formation,

---

[26] Smart phone.
[27] Said ad nauseam. We should apologize. Actually, Katy should, but I am complicit.
[28] I, Katy, had the fortune and misfortune of parenting my first child in the company of Foster Cline, one of the great parenting experts of the last century. He informed me that screens sabotage the industrious phase and doom me to a motherhood of "I'm bored, Mom!!" and thus would require me to entertain her because she failed to learn to entertain herself.

sculpting with playdough, making a leprechaun trap for St. Patrick's Day. Staring at a screen squanders the limited, precious time during this short developmental window, and instead of learning to *produce*, kids learn to *consume*.

When you *do* surrender to your teen,[29] cell phone training should follow the slow handoff method we cover at length in chapter 5.

- First *they watch you* manage your phone usage well. (Not dawn to dusk, neither oversharing nor undersharing on social media, using proper punctuation when you text goshdarnit.)
- Then *they help you* use your phone.[30] (You have them proof your text prior to tweeting; go through and delete photos with them and explain that even though you're killing it in your new bikini, that pic your dad took is not going on social media; you have them help you search Craigslist, and so forth.)
- When you give them their own phone, *you help them* navigate it. (Your email is connected to any of their accounts so notifications come to you. You review and approve any social media[31] contacts, take a hard line

---

[29] Do not do this in elementary school. Ever. If you give a middle schooler a phone, they just need text, phone, and maybe GPS. Utilize parental controls to cut them off at bedtime.

[30] I, Katy, do a lot of work in the car—at stop lights or hands-free dictation while I drive. Every one of my kids has served as my spell-checker and proofreader to make sure that Siri didn't make me sound like a moron. They have "helped" me draft professional emails, offer cheerful social media commentary, and even proofread texts for articles.

[31] Katy and I differ in opinion on social media. For the Manning kids, social media was a nonnegotiable hard no, and Mr. Manning would say this was one of the best parenting decisions we made. The Fausts were OK with monitored social media, and their kids are doing great. There is no one-size-fits-all recipe for success.

on only "friending" or "following" people they know in real life, set up the phone to require permission to download apps. Depending on the kid, remove access to internet browsers. Utilize every parental control available.)

- Finally, after a few years, *you watch them* use their phone responsibly.[32]

Mind you, when it comes to phones, the internet itself is not the primary danger; many of the resources we recommend in this book for you and your children are online. Further, a good internet filter can keep the vilest internet fodder at bay, and for good measure requiring that screen use be limited to the common areas of your home. It is social media, not the internet, that is your greatest foe and the primary online threat to your kids.[33] TikTok produced a COVID crop of girls who developed tics following overexposure to histrionic tic influencers. An autistic teen "realizes" they are trans after tumbling into a Reddit hole. There is mounting evidence that the use of screens in general, and of social media in particular, corresponds to higher and more severe rates of depression and

---

[32] No kid is perfect, especially with imperfect parents. We're all guilty of the occasional doom-scroll and playing too much Eight Ball.

[33] In a large UK sample of over seventeen thousand young people aged ten to twenty-one, researchers found the detrimental effects of high levels of social media use may be especially pronounced between ages fourteen–fifteen and nineteen for boys, and eleven–thirteen and nineteen for girls. Daria Kuss, "How Social Media Affects Children at Different Ages, and How to Protect Them," *phys.org*, April 1, 2022.

anxiety[34] as a result of overexposure[35] to the curated lives of their friends, which warps their sense of self and reality.

Give your kids the gift of a phone-free childhood. It's not just critical to raising conservative kids, but imperative to raising functional kids.

"Better a Year Too Early Than Five Minutes Too Late"

There is some subjectivity around the timing of talking with your kids about Woke ideas, and taking their maturity and sensitivity into account is important. That said, you should err on the side of sooner; as our people over at CanaVox often say, "Better a year too early than five minutes too late." For maximum impact you need to make some headway with every topic you're concerned about before they step foot into middle school. Unfortunately, this means you're generally broaching these subjects between first and third grades.

Here are a few examples of how to introduce some hot topics to your seven-year-old.

- "Everywhere you look there seems to be a screen, kiddo. There are many things on the internet that you cannot unsee and sometimes people put pictures or videos of naked people on the internet. That's called pornography, porn for short. Seeing it can make you

---

[34] "The data revealed the more time kids spent engrossed in digital screens, their symptoms of anxiety and depression became more severe." Tonya Mosley and Serena McMahon, "Social Media Use Linked to Anxiety, Depression among Teens, New Study Finds," WBUR Boston, January 20, 2019.

[35] The average tween clocks five hours of social media per day; the average teen, seven hours.

feel yucky. If you do see something like that, please tell me because it's important that we talk about it."

- "You know we love this country and believe it's a beacon of freedom for people across the world, but we haven't always lived up to American values. Did you know there was actually a time when black and white people had to have separate bathrooms by law? There was also a time when Chinese people couldn't become US citizens. In fact, during World War II our government put Japanese people in camps simply because they were Japanese. Our founding fathers had excellent ideas. But we have not always applied those ideals fairly. If you ever have questions about race or equality, I'm always open for that business."

- "You might hear the word transgender or "trans." It's a made-up word that means a person can become the opposite sex, which is impossible. Boys can't become girls, and girls cannot become boys. You are a boy, and boys, just like girls, have many different personalities. A boy that likes to do his sister's hair or loves to cook is still 100 percent boy. His interests don't determine whether he's a boy or a girl. His body does."

• • •

Katy here.

Admittedly, I didn't have these convos as early with my first child. She went to a private elementary school, and the world wasn't quite as insane a decade ago as it is today. We didn't introduce many of these topics until she was headed to a public middle school. My fourth child, Benjamin, on the other hand—six years her junior—has been privy to most conversations we've had with his elder siblings. Essentially, we got to him first by default, thankfully so, evidenced by the following exchange when he arrived home one day in third-grade:

Ben: *Today my teacher said that boys can wear dresses.*

Mom: *Oh, interesting. What do you think about that?*

Ben: *(pausing to consider) A boy can wear a dress, but that doesn't make him a girl.*

Mom: *Correct. Why not?*

Ben: *(long pause) He would have to change every cell in his body!*

The mild discomfort that they (or you) might feel when talking with your kids about socialism or cross-sex hormones or the KKK must be measured against the massive discomfort they'll experience if someone else shares this info with them, very likely in a way that will completely bulldoze their childhood innocence. Discomfort isn't your get-out-of-jail-free card.

Getting to your kid first is critical if you are serious about raising conservative kids. They *must* consider you the authority, and that means you *must* get to them first. But how can you fill them with good information if you don't have the right information yourself? You must become an expert because, as we discuss in the next chapter, when it comes to training, there's no special program in which you can enroll your kids that will save them from the world of the Woke. *You* are the Wokist repellant.

If your child is the ship, you are the harbor. While you do have the choice to keep them safe—physically and emotionally and ideologically sheltered—they're doomed if you send them unarmed and unprepared to face the leftist tempest they will surely encounter when they set sail. You must always keep foremost in your mind that you're not raising *children* to keep in your red-state harbor; you're training *adults* to launch into the stormy ocean blue. They need the skills to navigate predator-filled seas and the ability to adjust their bearings in changing social conditions. You cannot train them to sail properly unless you get to them first about the perils of open water. But before you can share proper navigation tactics, you need to understand them yourself.

CHAPTER 3

YOU ARE THE PROGRAM

All right, all right. We've kicked the dead horse enough. You get it. You understand that you can't keep your kids safe from the Woke world, but rather you must train them to navigate it. You're in. *But HOW?*

Well, buckle up, buttercup, because we've got The Solution for you. It's a simple, time-tested, one-size-fits-all hack that is guaranteed to deliver the anti-Woke results you seek.

We are living in an age of entitlement and instant gratification. Feeling sad? Here's a pill. Flat butt? Here's an implant. Don't want to read the assigned book? SparkNotes to the rescue. This shortcut mentality has turned our society into one that expects quick fixes, and in our customization to immediacy we've ended up short-cutting our way to the long road.

The "long road" is an ancient concept. The Talmud tells the story of Rabbi Yehoshua ben Hananiah asking a boy at the crossroads for directions to town. The boy replies, "This way is short but long, the other way is long but short." The first, while short in distance, is rife with obstacles. The second is a greater investment of travel time but absent the travails that may keep you from your destination entirely. In other words? The investment is worth it; do the work.

Naturally, this quick-fix mentality has also permeated parenting. Is there a book you can buy to protect them from the lies? A course that, upon completion, offers a certificate that will shield your kids from the Woke weapons? Some pill that will inoculate your kid against the Woke virus?

Yes. This magical fix-all is available immediately, and it's free. It's called P-A-R-E-N-T. *You are the irreplaceable anti-Woke program.*

There are helpful resources out there as you employ the PARENT training protocol. Organizations like MAVEN, Impact 360 Institute, and Summit Ministries offer camps and programs that inform your kids *what* to think and *why* to think it. There's also Worldview Academy,[1] which is the camp we have chosen to send our teens to every summer. But one week out of fifty-two ain't enough. *You* must be their Worldview Academy the other fifty-one.

Maybe all this cultural insanity has taken you by surprise—after all, we went from trans activists crying "we just need to pee" to the president of the United States endorsing the amputation and mutilation of children's healthy sex organs[2] seemingly overnight. It's easy to feel ill-equipped because most of us went into this parenting gig believing all our kids needed was food, shelter, and love, not a daily dissertation on

---

[1] Bitchin' teen apologetics camp where they spend a week among their people. They come home refreshed and informed.

[2] The actual meaning of "gender-affirming care."

the moral superiority of the free market. Sadly, that's exactly where we find ourselves these days.

Your assignment is to learn how to think and what to think about the insane cultural chaos *now* so you're equipped to instruct *them* when the time comes. You've got to know what you are *for* before you can teach your kids what they must be *against*. Knowing the *why*[3] behind the *what* is imperative to successfully teach your kids how to spot destructive lies and model gracious but firm resistance to Woke pressures in your relationships and workplace.

Become an Expert

Step one: **you must become an expert.**[4] We know, you're exhausted by work and carpool and filling out another ream of the same registration forms you filled out last year for every single activity. But if you don't want your children consumed by the Wokist mob, your self-education is a must. When it comes to socialism, abortion, gender ideology, critical race theory, revisionist history, and on...YOU need to have the facts straight. So, if you are ignorant, it's time to start walking the long road.

Of course, you can begin by reading great books. On the supremacy of the American system and the political climate of our time, we'd recommend Dennis Prager's *Still the Best Hope*, Ben Shapiro's *How to Destroy America in Three Easy*

---

[3]   The "God said it. I believe it. That settles it" approach never, not ever once, turned anyone in history toward Jesus.

[4]   OK. We don't mean *expert* expert. You just must know a whole lot more than your children do.

Steps,[5] and *Liberal Fascism* by Jonah Goldberg. On all matters of human design—abortion, marriage, transgender issues—Nancy Pearcey's *Love Thy Body* is a must. On topics of race, anything by Shelby Steele. On economics, anything by Thomas Sowell and Milton Friedman.

When it comes to social issues, CanaVox is one of the best resources. Join one of their reading groups to explore solutions to societal ills with like-minded adults. Start listening to the *BreakPoint* podcast daily—with your children if possible—for insight into deconstructing trending news from a biblical, rational worldview. For a deep dive into the founding of America and how to rightly view current events, check out the *WallBuilders* podcast. For daily political commentary, any one of the podcasters at Daily Wire gets an A+. Once you know how to critically think about and engage the culture, you can train your child to follow in your footsteps.[6]

Lamentably the best educational opportunities are often foisted upon you when Wokist absurdity bursts uninvited into your child's life.

• • •

Stacy here.

---

[5] *Reasons to Vote for Democrats* by Michael Knowles. Entirely blank, thus a very quick read.

[6] Note many of these resources skew Christian or are produced/authored by deeply religious folk. That's not a coincidence. Resisting Woke conformity requires fearing something more than the mob and must be combated with an accurate view of humanity, which both Judaism and Christianity provide. So, if you've rejected God, it might be time to reconsider that choice. You and your kids are going to need Him.

Thus began my education on Pacific Northwest tribal politics. We live just outside of Seattle, home to many native tribes. These tribes traffic in the white man's cash-money; their extraction method is predominantly by way of their supremely lucrative casinos. Another source of income for every nationally recognized tribe is tax money shelled out by the federal Bureau of Indian Affairs. Each state gets a dollar amount that's divvied up among the officially acknowledged tribes.

Many moons ago, Chief Sealth signed a treaty on behalf of the numerous tribes indigenous to the Puget Sound basin. This treaty ceded a territory called the Muckleshoot Prairie to this amalgam of tribes; thus, according to the treaty, these peoples became one federally recognized tribe called the Muckleshoot. One of the many tribes incorporated into this new tribe was the Duwamish people.

I know this because the librarian at my youngest's elementary school was opening each of her library Zoom classes with a "stolen land acknowledgment." Apparently, the descendants of the Duwamish want a share of the feds' cash and have been fighting unsuccessfully in the courts to be recognized as a separate tribe. What they've failed to accomplish in the courts, they are now attempting to do in the court of public opinion, and, of course, the indoctrinated public-school teachers are happily doing their part to brainwash the next generations on the tribe's behalf.

I had to do some homework, but it didn't take much investigation to understand the politics and money at the root of this propaganda campaign. My husband and I had many conversations around the dinner table with the kids about the "stolen land" nonsense and the story behind this new fad. When I did speak to the librarian, I was far better informed than she was on the subject matter. Politely, I explained that if she didn't have a grasp on the nuances of tribal infighting, how could second graders? Not to mention the immorality of telling my child he is guilty of stealing something he did not steal. Further, that humankind has been "stealing" land from one another from time immemorial, did she happen to know what people occupied the land before the Duwamish?

Thus ended the land acknowledgment, at least in Zoom school. However, once she was safely unobserved, back in her book fiefdom she was at it again.

Teachers Work for You

You are the primary educator of your children and teachers work for YOU. It's important to cultivate the mindset that teachers are contracted employees to whom you have outsourced the three Rs—reading, writing, and arithmetic—that's it. It's your job to teach the rest. Giving teachers a heads-up about the nature of your relationship at the beginning of the school year is helpful for all parties.

• • •

Stacy here.

Every September, whether via email or in person at the open house, I let my children's new teachers know that our family views my husband and me as the primary educators of our children and our children are well aware of our approach to education. I'm as gracious as possible in these communications, and I use language like "partnering in their education" and "team." But my explanation not-so-subtly puts them on notice as to what kind of Manning

Family Ambassador they're going to have in their class all year. The responses to my kind-but-clear communication have been very telling. Some teachers are beside themselves with appreciation to be dealing with parents who espouse such beliefs, but many have bristled. And if that's the response you get, be prepared and prepare your kid. Maybe the most important lesson that year, for both parent and child, will be learning how to deal with people with whom you disagree.[7]

Another important element of the teacher-parent relationships is positive communication. When your kid has an awesome teacher? Let that teacher know how much you appreciate them. People are people, and we all like to know when we are appreciated for the work we do. Making personal investments in teachers and staff at the schools is money in the bank for when you have to make a withdrawal in the form of a worldview pushback. Allies can be found at the schools; keep your eyes open for them.

. . .

Unfortunately, many teachers are opponents, not allies, when it comes to educating your children. Further, some don't have the intellectual mettle their multiple advanced degrees would indicate. On the training front, perhaps you've bought into the falsehood that "I can't teach my children, I'm not smart

---

[7]   It's also important to remember that not every left-leaning teacher is on a Woke mission. Very good teachers sometimes come in the form of a Democrat voter, and it's important to encourage these teachers and express your gratitude appropriately. Evelyn had an exceptional teacher who, oddly, the first time I met her, shared her pro-choice stance with me. I was taken aback and told Evelyn to be on alert, but I kept my powder dry. She's turned out to be a fantastic teacher and wrong about killing babies. Two things can be true at once.

enough," or "I don't have a teaching degree." Perhaps knowing that 75 percent of teacher prep programs don't even require a 3.0 GPA for entry and 12 percent have no academic standards for entry whatsoever[8] will free you from the belief that you're not qualified. On the whole, that statistic indicates that our kids are not being educated by the best and brightest. In fact, some of the indoctrination our kids are experiencing in schools is likely rooted in the teacher's inability to critically think about what they themselves have been taught.

• • •

Katy here.

Due to a missing graduation credit, compliments of COVID, Miriam was required to take both world history and US history during the same semester. Her father and I naively thought, "Excellent! History is so awesome!"[9]

Early on in her world history class, Miriam inquired, "What are we going to cover in this course? Mayans? Byzantine? Assyrians? Egyptians?"

Her Woke history teacher responded, "I usually let the kids decide. Generally, we focus on police brutality and LGBT rights."[10]

Miriam keeps her own counsel as a rule; she's not one for recreationally stirring the pot at school. So, she kept her head down and checked the necessary boxes until halfway through the year when both her world and US history teachers began simultaneously screening

---

[8]   "Teacher Prep Review Standard: Admissions," National Council on Teacher Quality, https://www.nctq.org/review/standard/Admissions.

[9]   Be advised: history is notoriously the Wokest of Woke subjects. Expect for your kids to be taught the exact opposite of the truth.

[10]   Cue *Price Is Right* too-bad-loser soundtrack.

the same "mass incarceration is an extension of slavery" documentary. Annoyed, Miriam, approached her world history teacher about it.

Mim: *Why are we watching this documentary? Aren't we supposed to be studying world history?*

Woke History Teacher: *US history is a part of world history.*

Mim: *Well, why am I watching the exact same documentary in two different classes that are supposed to have two different emphases?*

Woke History Teacher: *I'm sure we are evaluating it from different angles.*

Mim: *If you want to look at things from different angles, why don't you bring in different perspectives?*

Woke History Teacher: *Well, the documentary interviews a variety of people, so you are getting different perspectives.*

Mim: *This documentary presents one obvious narrative. Please tell me the distinct world history perspective I'm supposed to receive from your class that I'm not getting in my other class.*

Woke History Teacher: *Well, why don't you pay attention in both classes and then tell me.*

Mim: *Since you're the teacher I thought maybe you could tell me.*

Woke History Teacher: *You'll understand when you get to college. I can't wait for you to have this conversation with your college history teacher.*[11]

---

[11] So they can run you down like they did me? Pitch-perfect answer from a mind-numbed robot.

Miriam's high school history teacher obviously didn't know much about history, and her critical thinking ability was nonexistent. She dutifully regurgitated the talking points that her professors had spoon-fed her in college, lies that she apparently didn't question as she pursued her teaching degree. The Wokist lexicon spoken by this teacher is the same language that most of her peers and superiors speak. It surely served her well in her job interview, yet she couldn't hold her own when faced with the simple, honest questions of a teenage girl who smelled a rat.

To be fair, there *are* good public-school teachers out there who really are working hard to help kids excel academically. We know many between us; we love them and are grateful for their efforts. Some teachers have what it takes to educate your children. But so do you, with the added bonus that parents care more about your child's long-term thriving than any teacher ever could.

Customize Your Training Program

There is no shortcut to raising conservative kids in a hostile culture. There is also no standard-issue roadmap, and there shouldn't be. Every kid is different, and each will need a kid-specific training approach. This doesn't mean you need to reinvent your tactics with each kid; it means rigid rules are not necessary, which is freeing.

If you have a bleeding heart–type daughter, you'll need to emphasize that dishonesty (e.g., honoring someone's requested delusional pronouns) is never loving. If you have a slash-and-burn type son, drive home the truism that most of the time, people won't care how much you know about anything until they know you care about them.[12] If you have an introvert-type child, don't expect them to take regular public stands but do expect them to stand firm. If you have a loud-mouth know-it-all,[13] remind them that being "quick to listen, slow to speak, and slow to anger"[14] has been the approach of righteous men and women for two thousand years. Maybe you have a bossy-type who would revel in leading a weekly dinner table discussion on trending news. Perhaps you and your musical kid write a rock ballad, *Hamilton* style. And if you have an advanced reader who is curious about the political world around her? You tell her to read *The Hunger Games*.[15]

• • •

Stacy here.

Evelyn exited the womb a voracious reader. She was one of those kids who would mispronounce advanced vocabulary words because she'd only seen them in written form. To say she read above grade level in elementary school is a gross understatement. It was because of her advanced comprehension, and possibly my questionable judgment, that I assigned her The Hunger Games *series to read during the summer between second and third grade.*

---

12 Turn-of-phrase silliness for relationship matters most if you have any hope of influencing someone.
13 Like Stacy, God help that woman.
14 God, forgive her.
15 Has anyone called Child Protective Services yet?

I'd read the series myself, and I thought it was an excellent exploration of tyranny, politics, and class warfare. Evelyn was deeply affected by it. We had many predictable conversations about all the ways Washington, DC, and Hollywood were the real-life Capitol City, and how important it is to do the right thing even when it's costly. I was most taken with her assessment of the series heroine, Katniss Everdeen. Evelyn noticed and appreciated that Katniss relied on tools and her mind to survive the games, not brute force or "girl power." She also appreciated that the heroine was written in a way that conformed to all observable facts about the physical differences between the sexes, differences we'd been honoring and enforcing throughout her young life. Reading The Hunger Games *was not appropriate for the oldest Manning male at the same developmental stage and would emotionally damage the youngest male, who is older now than his sister was at the time. We assigned this to Evelyn specifically because, well, Evelyn.*

• • •

C. S. Lewis came from a wealthy family who hired a tutor to provide his education. Following his academic assessment, the tutor reported his findings to Lewis's father. According to the version of the story we're retelling, the tutor explained that C. S. struggled with math but was a natural with language; therefore, they would focus on literature.[16]

Good trainers see strengths and customize training programs. Effectively training your children in conservatism is no different. You know your kid best, which means you are the

---

[16] Which totally worked out for C. S.

ideal person to identify fun, memorable, engaging ways to bring conservative principles to life. You know what kind of information stimulates them and the ideal kid-specific delivery system.

If you embrace the role of *program* for your child, you won't need to spend eight hours deprogramming them from the seven they spent at school because you've equipped them with the skills needed to recognize the lies and propaganda. When you create kid-specific conservative training, they will start to see the truths that you are communicating come alive. Your kids will come home and report the crazy goings on in school, they'll ask you questions and send you mid-day texts with snapshots of outrageous assignments so you can help them or laugh with them. When you are the program in which your kids are enrolled, they become naturally skeptical of any information that gives them that HMMMmmmmm feeling. They begin to fact-check on their own and when they're still unsure, they turn to you for the truth. And if *you're* unsure? You seek the truth together.

In this book, we are going to share some tips on the *when*, the *how*, and the *what* to educate your kids about at various ages. But the *who* never changes. It's you. You are the program. While we can offer some guiding principles, YOU know your kids; we don't. That is why parents are the primary educators, because a great education is tailored to each child—their interests, maturity, leanings—and you know those better than anyone else. You also have the superpower of being the most connected to, protective of, and invested in your child. You care about them more than any teacher ever will. It's you, not their fifth-grade teacher Mrs. Jenkins,[17] who is there when they succeed or fail.

When it comes to conservative parenting, you are the optimal training program. But proper training requires ongoing communication. And there will be little to no effective communication unless you master the "no-flinch" rule.

---

[17] According to her email signature, Mrs. Jenkins identifies as She/Her. Eye roll.

CHAPTER 4

NO-FLINCH RULE

Throughout the parenting saga, and especially if you're raising culture warriors, you are going to be subject to a boatload of infuriating, triggering nonsense. The following are some fairly vanilla examples of what today's parents are met with when their kiddos arrive home from school, shared with us by fellow moms out here in Seatt-hell's[1] trenches fighting the good fight:

- "Why is there a boy running with the girls in the track meet?"
- "My friend said he's nonbinary. Does that mean he's not a boy or a girl?"
- "A mean girl in class said I needed to shut up about abortion because I have a penis."
- "My teacher made us say the Black Lives Matter pledge."
- "Mom, there was this girl at the park whose dad kept calling her 'they.'"

---

[1] Also known as the Emerald Sh*tty.

43

- "My teacher made Alex cry in class today. She told him he's the reason for all the problems in America because he's a 'white cis male.'"
- "There's one American flag outside my school, but there's a rainbow flag in all my classrooms."
- "Three of my friends are 'pan' and in a throuple. What does that even mean?"
- "I have three Muslim classmates who leave class several times a day to pray, but they won't let me start an afterschool bible club."

It's very tempting to go off like an A-bomb, "are you F-ing KIDDING me!?!" style, after your kid reports that his teacher proclaimed, "If you are a Republican, you are racist" in class. You could respond with a this-one-goes-to-eleven-volumed *"What the CUSS? YOU'RE IN THIRD GRADE. Seriously, WHY can't they just teach you reading, writing, and arithmetic?!? God in heaven, help me find my coat because I'm going to march over to that godforsaken school and tell that gosh-darn troublemaker[2] teacher what's what. I-tell-you-what, there's NO WAY that teacher looks me in the eye and spews that hateful garbage to my face. But to my defenseless eight-year-old? Flipping inexcusable. These cussing people are driving me insane."*

Such a reaction, of course, is right and proper. Each example of the Woke insanity we listed above is nonsensical, outrageous, and/or unjust, and the "are you F-ing KIDDING me!?!"

---

[2]   I, Stacy, preferred "asshat" but apparently that's name-calling, and, as Katy has to remind me on the reg, we don't attack people—we attack ideas. I submit that *behaving like an asshat* would have split that hair carefully enough, but Katy's a hard-ass. Rather, *she behaves* like a hard-ass.

A-bomb rant is both natural and satisfying in the moment. Railing rant-style against the teacher or the school or the insane cultural everything does help dissipate some of your white-hot rage. But, upon hearing something ridiculous or shocking, parents who prioritize training must *keep their cool*. Even as your brain is melting from righteous indignation, your face needs to remain serene. This is what we call the *No-Flinch rule*, and it's a critical parenting strategy for raising kids who can effectively fight the culture war.

We have not employed the No-Flinch rule perfectly throughout our parenting sagas; as a matter of fact, No-Flinch was known by the far less elegant moniker of WHATEVER YOU DO STAY CALM AND DON'T FREAK OUT rule before we learned of this improved name while discussing the importance of maintaining a game face when your kid asks, "Mom, what's an anal plug?" when our mutual friend overheard our discussion and piped in, "Hey, that's the No-Flinch rule!" Well, of course it is. Apparently, a seasoned couple at our friend's church had been teaching parents about this easy-to-say, hard-to-do principle for decades.[3]

The No-Flinch rule is an important principle for every parent, but it's a nonnegotiable for those of us who wish to raise conservative kids in a hostile world. Why is that? Because you will not be able to transmit your values unless there is *constant communication* between parents and kids. If your default is to scream, rage, gasp, or flinch, they're more likely to keep the Woke shenanigans to themselves which doesn't bode well

---

[3] If you're not a church type, you might want to rethink that.

for training up conservatives. The No-Flinch rule will help impart your worldview in the following ways:

• • •

Receptivity. You'll be doing an inordinate amount of teaching on the long road of conservative parenting. You'll be saturating your kids in truth during elementary school, introducing them to challenging concepts in middle school, and staying connected to high schoolers. During literal-homeroom[4] instruction, your kid will be passively absorbing information or listening to you preach from your soapbox.[5] Chalk up a win on the parenting scoreboard when your eyes bore into them mid-*Stranger Things* sex scene and they roll their eyes in teen-drama fashion and offer a "Yes, Mom, I know they glossed over the pregnancy risk and depression Nancy will face post hookup." Such a response to mom's piercing-gaze-quiz is a sign that the running dialogue is having the right effect; you are teaching, and they are absorbing.

Lectures are great, we're big fans, but the real headway is made when they *want* to listen to you. That generally isn't the case during parental I-speak/you-listen-diatribes. Kids are *really* listening when you are providing answers to their genuine questions. Say you've got no choice but to run an errand to drug-infested, homeless-encampment-filled downtown,[6] and *they* ask *you*, "Mom, why is that man leading that other

---

4   You see what Stacy did there? She is too clever by half.
5   Captive audiences are our favorites.
6   Godspeed if that's Portland for you.

man around by a leash?"[7] That's the moment when they're hungriest for information. What you say, and how you say it, right after they ask you an honest, often urgent question, is what they're likely to file away as the most important thing to remember. It's your chance to connect the dots between a real-time situation and the conservative truths you've been pouring into them. If you flinch, you risk forfeiting the most ripe of teachable moments.

It's our opinion that teens are the smartest stupid people on the planet. This manifests by way of young people who listen but do not hear, usually because they aren't asking but being told. Many times, we both have been surprised by a question from our kids that they *very much should* know the answer. It is just as important to employ the no-flinch rule in such circumstances as it is when they bring you a jaw-dropper. Having your kid ask if they should wash their hands before they help you cook dinner is exasperating and ridiculous, but just saying yes is better than relationship-damaging eye rolls and a barrier-building raised voice. When you handle the silly stuff with grace, you, not the Google,[8] will be the one they consult when they want to know what cutting is.

. . .

---

[7] "Everyone will serve something, little Jimmy. Our family serves God. Those men have made their feelings their god, and it has led them to a very obvious and degrading kind of enslavement."

[8] Of course we know it's singular. And the Googles is not the. Neither is the Costcos. We don't care. We likes it that way.

Katy here.

Last month, Josh, my fifteen-year-old asked me, "Mom, what's Watergate?" I silently reeled, "How could you have spent nine years in school, not to mention grown up under this roof, without knowing what Watergate is!?!?" No doubt he'd heard the term at least a dozen times, whether in passing on a podcast or by overhearing his father and me use words like Russiagate or Pizzagate at the dinner table when discussing current events. Looking at his face, my assumption was obviously erroneous. Thankfully, I'd perfected my flinch-free face with my first two kids, so I didn't bat an eye. Instead of responding in a way that might have made him think "I must be an idiot, I'll just Google it next time," we did a quick Nixon recap, which led me to introduce Chuck Colson,[9] which naturally flowed into a discussion on the ways God's word can produce a bumper crop of fruit when it lands in fertile soil. The fact that it was he who was seeking an answer, rather than another mom lecture, meant he was hyper-focused and retained the information...and then some.

Train yourself to not explode on your kids to keep from squandering their most teachable moments.

• • •

No barriers. Becoming the go-to person who can be asked a n y t h i n g is one of the most critical factors for success when it comes to raising kids in general, and raising conservative

---

9   Known as Nixon's "hatchet man," Colson participated in Watergate and then converted to Christianity. He then voluntarily pleaded guilty to obstruction charges, spent seven months in prison, founded the largest prison reform ministry in the country, and became one of the twentieth century's great Christian apologists. According to one biographer, "He transferred his huge drive, intellect and maniacal energy from the service of Richard Nixon to the service of Jesus Christ."

kids specifically. It is therefore essential to establish yourself as their safe space when they need to process challenging, complex, or controversial issues. This can be especially problematic[10] when the culture, their peers, and the media echo the message that parents are untrustworthy, out-of-touch troglodytes—in other words, The Enemy. Getting to your kids first can mitigate some of the Woke anti-parent messages.

But the Woke aren't the only ones who can erect barriers between you and your kids. If, because of your unpredictable explosiveness, they view potentially upsetting conversations with you as burdensome, you will do the Wokists' bidding by erecting barriers on their behalf. Even if your anger or outrage is not directed at them, when you cannot control your fury, you may unintentionally trigger their fight-or-flight response and deter them from future interactions with you. Your immediate response after your high schooler tells you that a friend gave her some rice crispy treat and fifteen minutes later she realized it was an edible will train your kid to either run *to you* or run *from you* when they need you most.

In those moments of confession or processing, your kid has their own emotions to deal with—they don't need the additional burden of yours. For example, when your fifth-grade daughter tells you that her girlfriend has a crush on her and wants to date her, she's trying to process her own discomfort and confusion. But if she's been conditioned to expect she'll have to endure your "damn this sick culture" emotional diatribe before she gets answers, connection, or emotional

---

[10]   We're on a mission to repatriate Woke vocabulary.

clarity, there's a good chance that she'll choose someone else with whom to process—like her teacher, her friends, or the internet. And unless you began reading this book at the top of this paragraph, you already know that those are exactly the sources you *do not* want her turning to. The other option is that she talks to no one about her internal life, and the instinct that tells her "this isn't right" begins to fade...or, worse, controls her.

Having a barrier-free relationship with your child is important for conservative parenting. It's also important for parenting in general. A mutual friend of ours, who happens to be killing it in the parenting game, shared a weighty No-Flinch win with us a few years back. We've asked her permission to include the story anonymously because of its highly sensitive nature. Here's what happened.

While this mom-friend sat folding laundry in her bedroom, her husband and their youngest daughter were busy with a woodworking project in dad's shop. With seemingly no impetus, as reported by her husband, their daughter drops a "The neighbor boy touched my private parts" stunner[11] on her dad. We know this father to be the fiercely protective, sensitive type—a real feeler. His lizard brain said scream and rage, to cry and demand she tell him every detail before he stormed out the door to confront the offender. Instead, in a moment of No-Flinch excellence, he mastered his innate desire for immediate retribution and let some time pass; he then excused himself and sought out his laundry-folding wife. After shutting their door, he screamed and raged and punched pillows, and

---

[11]   Stunner is inadequate. More an OH MY GOD I'VE FAILED YOU—I AM HOMICIDAL—JESUS HELP ME vibe.

when he had calmed down a bit, choking back his tears, he recounted the details of their daughter's revelation. Then he and his wife formulated a plan to consult law enforcement, meanwhile getting as much information about the incident as possible from their daughter. Game-face firmly affixed, he returned to the workshop and said, "Thanks for letting me know about what happened with the neighbor kid. Can you tell me more about that?" His serene tone signaled that he was a safe place to deposit even the most uncomfortable details about a situation that demanded confrontation and accountability.

The moral of the story? It's not your child's job to manage your emotions, children are not your rage-release valve. For the most communicative, open relationship with your kid, emotional release needs to be a one-way street, headed in your direction. The No-Flinch rule prioritizes your child's intellectual and emotional needs above your urge to blow up.[12]

· · ·

Become a refuge. It's a hostile culture, classroom, neighborhood, and friend zone, that's why you need to be the go-to for conversation in your kid's world. When your daughter proclaims that she was "assigned female at birth" and your response is to calmly inquire, "Is sex assigned or observed?", she learns that Mom and Dad can handle whatever she brings to you. Your kids may not be able to say "all lives matter" on the playground, and they self-censor during classroom

---

[12] You will fail at times. It's OK.

discussions about illegal immigration. But because you've mastered[13] the No-Flinch rule, they know that they can ask Mom and Dad about the merits or risks of gun control or a friend's name and pronoun change, even if (especially if) they're not sure what they themselves think about it. You are their refuge, the best place to ask big questions, process aloud, and express doubt without fear of ostracization.

It's inevitable that your young culture warriors will have some epic fails along the way, so keeping your dismay from making its way to your expression is a flinch-free skill that is also valuable to refine.[14] These are especially painful in the early years when their little brains work in a more binary, black-and-white manner.[15] But if you've laid the No-Flinch foundation, it will be in *you* that he confides his failure and *you* will be the one to help him find his way back from a rash "All illegal immigrants crossing the southern border are murderers and rapists" after he blindly lashed out in response to a mob of Woke classmates.

Consistently applying the No-Flinch rule means your kid will associate you not only with good information but also with the love-instilling bonus of peace and relief. Other than opening the channels of worldview conversation, the No-Flinch rule has the critical ancillary benefit of incentivizing confessions of incriminating or even disturbing information. Maybe

---

[13] More likely failing at times but striving to be as no-flinchy as possible.

[14] The unforced errors committed by Stacy's eldest have been north of epic. Hair-graying, house-afire, "Wait, you said what?!?!"'s

[15] For example: "We love cousin Andrew, but boys shouldn't wear dresses." "So Andrew is bad?" "No, we just disagree with his choices." "So you're saying Andrew is bad..."

they cheated on a history test, witnessed their friend shoplift, or found themselves stuck at a party where there wasn't supposed to be drinking. In these situations, rationally or irrationally, their fear of punishment may keep them from seeking your counsel. But if you have a consistent No-Flinch practice, they intuitively know that they *always feel relief* after a bout of honesty with you, even if they must face negative consequences.

Many times more than you'd rather, their confession *does* result in drafting an apology letter to their history teacher, having to establish boundaries with a friend, or suffering a stricter curfew. But children thrive when clear boundaries and expectations are enforced, even when it's costly to them. Enforcing boundaries in concert with the No-Flinch rule means that it'll be easier for them to connect their own poor choices to consequences, rather than seeing consequences as Mom's flinchy, irrational, rage-fueled punishment. No-flinch parenting demonstrates that your kid can come to you with anything, even if they're confused, have said the wrong thing, or know that consequences must follow. You are their safe space, and a safe space is a calm place.

· · ·

Aim your rage at the right target, just make sure your kid isn't downrange. The aim of the No-Flinch rule is to reduce friction between your child's questions or confessions and your appropriate assurances. But, to clarify, No-Flinch is not the same as deadpan. You will need to show an appropriate emotional response when your fifth grader reports that Mr. Grayson "came out" to the class, and express horror that she[16] regaled her students with graphic details of her double mastectomy. A horror that turns to sadness as you discuss how awful it is that someone was so deeply disturbed, they thought mutilating their body would bring them happiness, and anger at the doctors who took advantage of her confused mind for a paycheck. The emotion you display communicates that your kid was right to be uncomfortable.

The revelation that the middle school held a "privilege walk,"[17] which meant all the straight, "cis" white boys had to sit in the back of the classroom for a week, should be met with disgust. While spending five days sitting in the last row with the other deplorables did mean he got some respite from teacher oversight for the week, he knew it wasn't right. Your properly directed anger, followed by a team writing effort to the administration expressing that the "privilege walk" was anathema to the principles Martin Luther King Jr. and Rosa Parks fought for, validates his own anger and builds trust in his own instincts.

An adult's failure to model and reflect the appropriate emotional response to injustice means children will be less sensitive to it themselves. The child-abuse victims most likely to experience lasting trauma are those who never had an adult mourn, rage, and take action on their behalf when they learned of the abuse. For example, if Mom's response to

---

[16] We don't misgender. Period.

[17] If we were talking about the only actual privilege that exists for children, an intact home, then sure. Privileged beyond measure.

learning that Uncle Jed had little Johnny sleep nude with him in his sleeping bag on their camping trip "for warmth" is "My brother would never do such a thing—you're lying"? The likelihood that Johnny will suffer long-term abuse and believe he was in the wrong for reporting it is high.

That's because, when children have been wronged or treated unjustly, their small internal voice whispers, *This isn't right*. But until they see their gut response reflected by some downright biblical wailing and gnashing of adult teeth, kids don't know whether or not to trust that internal whisper. Johnny's got to see his mother's rage while she reports her brother's crime to the police for his instincts to be validated and for him to recognize future abuse.

You recall that woodworking father mentioned previously? After he calmly absorbed his daughter's revelation, she witnessed him cry in grief and sadness because he had not protected her from the world, then she watched as he confronted the neighbor boy in swift order, and then her father (in cooperation with his parents) oversaw the boy's confession and repentance to her. She watched as her dad establish a hard boundary, which he made crystal clear to all parties, *would not be crossed*. She benefited greatly from seeing her own unease reflected in her dad's response and the swift and serious action he took on her behalf. This example of a parent processing his own rage without burdening his kid with it is a perfect illustration of a parent standing firmly at the end of the emotional one-way street.

Young children's inability to properly contextualize their surroundings is one of the many reasons why exposing them to things like drag queen story hour is so damaging. If you've ever watched footage of this type of child abuse, you'll see that witnessing faux-cleavage-bearing, fishnet-stockinged, mini-skirt-adorned[18] men twerking at the public library induces expressions of uncertainty and fear in the under-five crowd. If little Dr. Seuss–aged Ava's discomfort is not mirrored by her mother,[19] who instead is smiling and cheering the perverts on, it sends the message that *she, the preschooler,* is wrong for feeling uncomfortable by this hypersexualized lady-faced clown. If, on the other hand, Mom unwittingly took Ava to the library during groomer story time and she responds by quickly scooping her up, apologizing for her mistake, and declaring that adults should never behave that way in front of children, it validates Ava's internal sense of alarm, which gives Ava a better shot at identifying future predatory situations and escaping victimization.

Alarming circumstances and disturbing statements are seemingly endless when you are raising conservative kids in a Woke world. The challenge is to ensure that the teacher or the YouTuber or the destructive lies are the clear target of your ire, not the child who's reporting them. The No-Flinch rule will help instill in your conservative child that you are a

---

[18] Every single one of these lady-face drag types missed every episode of *What Not to Wear*. Real women know, or learned from *WNTW*, that miniskirts are verboten after age thirty-five.

[19] It is abusive for any adult, especially a child's own parents, to subject their children to overtly debased sexual content. Such parents deserve to be publicly shamed and ostracized from civil society.

partner and confidante in this war on the Woke. Flinch-free parenting goes a long way toward opening the communication channels crucial to each phase of the next chapter's slow handoff strategy.

CHAPTER 5

←——————————————→

THE SLOW HANDOFF

Woke cities are governed by bad ideas. One example of a very bad idea here in Washington State is the law that allows thirteen-year-old children the power to make medical decisions for themselves, without input from their parents. Adding insult to injury, these laws require the parent-funded insurance plans to pay, and therefore the parents to co-pay, for procedures and treatments that "doctors" cannot lawfully reveal to the payors, known also as the parents. So, here in the Evergreen State, those policies result in parents having to *ask their child's permission* to bear witness to the entirety of their doctor visits.

• • •

Katy here.

This is the appalling circumstance in which I found myself last year during my then fifteen-year-old daughter's sports physical. Since we are hemmed in by Wokists in this godforsaken place, I'm forced to be aware of these laws, thus I gave Miriam the heads-up about what to expect at the clinic. I informed her that it was her choice as to whether I would remain in the exam room. If she wanted me there, I would insist on staying. Narrowing her gaze, she pursed her lips and replied, "I've got this, Mom."

After the rudimentary height, weight, and medical history portion of the exam, the doctor turned to me and explained, "I'm going to need to have you step out now, Mom." To which I responded, "That's my daughter's decision." I asked her if she consented to meet with the doctor alone. She replied, "No problem." So out I stepped. About a minute later, the doctor invited me to return. On the way home Miriam regaled me with the juicy details of their verbal joust:

Doc: *(adopting a "finally we can speak frankly" tone)* "So, how many sexual partners do you have?"

Mim: "None."

Doc: *(code-switching to skepticism)* "OK. Are you doing drugs or alcohol?"

Mim: "No I'm not. Now, can I ask you some questions?"

Doc: *(expression softening as Mim is obviously gearing up to "tell her truth" now that she's in a safe space, away from her mommy)* "Of course."

Mim: "If I was having sex or doing drugs, would you tell me to stop?"

Doc: *(visibly crestfallen)* "Well, only if it was a problem."

Mim: "Isn't it always risky for teens to be having sex and doing drugs and drinking alcohol?"

Doc: (realizing he's brought a knife to a gunfight) "Sometimes we can give them things to help."

Mim: "If kids are involved in dangerous activities, shouldn't you tell their parents? Shouldn't the parents be the ones helping kids? After all, it's the parents who are there for their kids in the long run, not you."

Doc: "I think we are done here." (Enter Momma Bear, stage Far Right.)

As I basked in the glow of this parenting win, I took an epic mental victory lap. Not only had she stood her ground, but she'd also pushed back.[1] But this win did not materialize overnight; teens like Miriam, capable of standing firm and confidently challenging aggressive adults or the damaging worldviews held by their peers, takes cultivation. It requires methodical training from early childhood before you get to enjoy watching them intrepidly take on the Woke.

· · ·

The training method recommended in this book is based on the concept of replication, and its success hinges on you becoming an expert; thus, it is essential to have drunk the Kool-Aid we've served up in the previous chapters. When you understand that you are training children to understand what they are *for* and *why* they are for it, that you must get to them first, that you will unflinchingly face challenges with them,

---

[1] Cue throngs of cheering imaginary onlookers.

and that *you* are the program in which your child is enrolled, the process of value replication can commence.

The Process of Replication

> "You teach what you know,
> but you reproduce what you are."
> –Howard Hendricks

In this chapter, we'll explain our training method[2] and give examples of how you can reproduce your values in your children. This formula is applicable to any skill you want your child to master, whether carpentry or baking or defending their values. It's the method we have both used to develop capable, confident conservative kids.

---

[2]   We are not responsible for developing this concept. Katy saw this on a discipleship website many moons ago, and it left a powerful impression, likely because truth does have a certain ring to it.

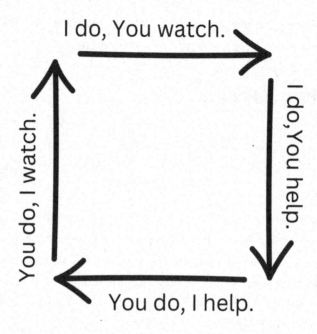

Step 1. I do, you watch.
Step 2. I do, you help.
Step 3. You do, I help.
Step 4. You do, I watch.

This simple formula mirrors a child's natural physical and emotional development, it succinctly describes what we'll call the slow handoff parenting technique. This approach requires you to view all activities, even the mundane, as a training platform. We know it's often easier to keep the kids otherwise occupied while you go about your business, but it is in the day-to-day, where the foundational training is poured. We will illustrate this training method with a lesson in laundry, admittedly a more easily replicated skill than is refuting a Marxist worldview.

Laundry Step 1: "I do the laundry; you watch me do the laundry." This is the easy part, so easy that some moms never get beyond this step.[3]

Until they are four or five years old, your kids will watch you do laundry.[4] You add the proper measure of soap, you start the cycle, you fold the socks. The "you watch" of Step 1 is descriptive. You'll explain what you're doing while they watch. "First, if I'm feeling fancy, I sort for textures and colors. Then, I put the laundry in the washing machine and add the soap. The machine adds water when I push this button."

Laundry Step 2: "I do the laundry, you help me do the laundry" commences around age five or six. The "you help" of Step 2 is prescriptive. You instruct them in sock-balling techniques. You show them how to measure the detergent. They push the start button. You have them clean out the lint trap. Step 2 lasts a few years, and over its course, not every load will require the same treatment, which necessitates explanations of how the rules of laundry may change based on different fabrics and load sizes. Special circumstances, like not washing red with whites or the fact that their father is very uptight about the way his pants are hung to dry, so much so that you

---

[3] This mom makes chicken tendies and Pop-Tarts for her basement-dwelling, Peter Panish man-child while he dorks out on video games, dooming him to produce significantly less testosterone than his peers and damning his chances to successfully launch.

[4] Mountains of it, hundreds and hundreds of soul-sucking loads of it.

can't even do it correctly, will teach them to observe nuance and circumstance.[5]

Years eight to ten usher in Laundry Step 3: "You do the laundry, I help." At this stage, you transfer the primary responsibility of laundering to them. You might remind them to start a load, but a reminder is all the assistance they get from you. Responsibility for having clean underwear means they'll get serious about laundry duties right quick. You can bend on flipping their clothes from the washer to the dryer if they ask you for help, but you don't offer. Try to fold the laundry together twice a week if you can; it's during these routine moments that you can make meaningful connections with your kids. Some of the best worldview conversations take place when you're working side by side, especially with boys who notoriously do not volunteer for face-to-face conversation.

By the time they are twelve to fourteen years old, Laundry Step 4—they are doing, and you are watching—should be in full swing. Congratulations, you've unleashed a laundry authority on the world.

For this strategy to flourish, you yourself must be an expert in laundering.[6] But you have to know what you're doing and *why* you do it.

The takeaway from our laundry scenario is that you don't exist to be their perpetual laundress; you use this method to *train* your kids to do their own laundry. *You* are their laundry program. A YouTube rabbit hole on handwashing vs. cotton/

---

5   And that daddy maybe takes the laundry a tad too seriously.
6   Not an expertise that rises to the level of competently hang-drying your husband's pants, mind you; that kind of prowess requires a laundry savant.

sturdy can't hold a candle to including your kids in a multiyear education in laundering.[7] Because you "got to them first" on checking clothing tags, they will come to you, not the Google, with questions about washing delicates.

As you incrementally assign them bite-size pieces of the job, expect them to fail, but do not freak out when they do. This is the type of low-risk activity in which you cultivate that No-Flinch response when they confess they've hot-washed a dry-clean-only item. This builds trust with your kids and hopefully results in greater approachability when something more consequential is afoot than turning a white sweater pink. Staying connected, no matter what the trial, will help to ensure you're the one they come to when they've God-forbid-a-thousand-times put their father's pants in the dryer or when they discover their friend is considering abortion.

So what does the slow handoff approach look like when it comes to inculcating conservative values?

Step 1 will commence in the years spanning ages two to ten. Your kid will witness you consuming all the resources, and more, that we mentioned in chapter 3. Observing you becoming an expert is a sizable portion of Step 1 in their worldview training—they are watching you read, listen to, and grapple with conservative ideas. You are becoming an expert; they are watching. Two birds—one stone.

Throughout these early years, you perfume the household airways with humorous conservative commentary such as *The*

---

[7] YouTube is a censorious tool of the Democrat machine. They might own this corner of the internet for now, but do your part to end their tyranny by using the free-speech platform Rumble.com whenever possible.

Andrew Klavan Show. Your kids have witnessed you calmly, but firmly, engage with dissenters in person and online. They've heard you say, "That's a good question; I'm not sure. Can I get back to you after I've had some time to think on this?" when the holier-than-thou Prius-driving neighbor whose tailgate is covered with lefty stickers like RESIST, NEVER FORGET JANUARY 6th and I'M WITH HER asks you to prove that the Second Amendment actually allows citizens to own cannons.[8] And they've seen you survive the real-life fallout of speaking truth that is unpopular.

Modeling is the essence of Step 1. You are *doing*, and they are *watching*. "We become what we behold,"[9] so if you want your children to "become" experts who can stand firm on conservative values, they must "behold" you consistently living it. Step 1 is all about your kids seeing you seek knowledge and wisdom and letting them witness you discuss worldview topics during their preschool and elementary school years.

Around middle school—and even younger for more curious, mature, or let's face it, female children—you need to initiate Step 2: *I do, you help.* You keep on with what you are already doing, but it's now time to look for ways that they can help you do it.

Perhaps, for example, you decide that instead of eating a nice big bowl of rusty nails, you'd rather engage in a futile Twitter spat over whether critical race theory (CRT) is being

---

[8]   It was today-o'clock when Katy learned that her right to own a cannon was constitutionally protected. Thank heavens Mrs. Manning is part of this writing project.

[9]   John M. Culkin, "A Schoolman's Guide to Marshall McLuhan," *Saturday Review*, March 18, 1967, 51–53.

taught in our schools. Since you've already stepped in it,[10] you might as well turn your poor choice into a "you help" moment. Invite your tween to read over your exchanges and discuss your opponent's objections with them. Search for articles written by CRT expert Neil Shenvi and have your kid read it aloud while you do the dishes. Ask your mini-me to suggest edits to your "the schools refuse to label what they're teaching as CRT, but their actions are lockstep with the Marxist formula of utopia advocacy, structural critique, and enlisting students as foot soldiers in their war on manufactured wrongs" response.

Maybe your kid witnessed your poster-child-for-the-left mother-in-law successfully bait you into another heated, socially awkward debate at your niece's birthday party on the growing threat of white supremacists. On the car ride home, talk to your kids about how you could have better communicated your thoughts in order to persuade those listening[11] to your "conversation." Point out that Grandma always frames her debates in terms of the oppressed and the oppressors because she's operating from a Marxist worldview and discuss what kind questions you could ask to get her thinking about the world from the perspective of individual merit instead of group identity, assuming she insists on another row at the family reunion.

If they've been *watching* you *do* on worldview topics and have *helped* you engage in challenging conversations, Step 3 will commence naturally. A telltale sign that this transition has

---

[10] For you sheltered readers, the "it" to which we refer is a pile of fecal matter.
[11] Sometimes you're using a debate to convince onlookers, not to persuade your opponent.

begun is when they jump in and slam the car door, launching into a tirade about their teacher's claim that support for gay marriage is the same as supporting interracial marriage.[12] Or you'll know the switch has flipped when the picture they text you of their history assignment to "draft a more equitable constitution" is followed by 👹 🧠 🦠 ⚫ 🐷. At this point they are savvy enough to spot the Woke, but they aren't yet equipped enough to rebut the teacher without your help.

• • •

Katy here.

During his fifth-grade year in Zoom[13] school, my youngest, Benjamin, was subjected to "Black Lives Matter" week. This kid is a hammer looking for a nail, and BLM week promised a host of nails to pound. He'd already been rebuked for asking why there wasn't a designated week for any other people group, and he knew that there was going to be social pressure for non-black students to confess that they were racist. We strategized about how he could complete the assignments without violating his convictions, and I promised to help him.

The teacher showed a video comparing the civil rights movement of the 1960s with the current day fight against "systemic racism." The class was then assigned to write a short essay explaining what they are personally going to do to fight racism today. I asked

---

[12] Them Before Us Sparknotes: Kids in interracial marriages have access to 100 percent of their biological identity and the mothering and fathering that maximizes child development. Kids in gay marriages lose 50–100 percent of their biological identity and often hunger for their missing mom or dad. Interracial marriage grants children wholeness; gay marriage requires child loss.

[13] Will Zoom ever be able to shake the stench of COVID? Doubtful.

Ben to draft his three main points, which were "I am a Christian and I believe God made all races equal," "God hates injustice so that means all injustice," and "I need to stand up for anyone who's being bullied regardless of their race." Then we discussed how Martin Luther King Jr., who was quoted in the video, appealed to the same moral authority[14] Benjamin does. We added some great MLK quotes about equality, and his conclusion was that his faith is what drives him to uphold justice.

Ben completed the assignment without compromising his convictions. His nervousness before hitting the "submit" button paled in comparison to the pride he felt when the teacher read his answer in front of the whole class. I couldn't have engineered a better "you do, I help" kickoff.

• • •

Step 3 done correctly looks like this: Your middle-schooler reports that his class discussion was based on the precept that antebellum South slaveholders must've been Republicans because Republicans are racist. You neither flinch nor pound out an angry email to the teacher but instead ask your son to watch a video on the history of the Democratic Party with you[15] or have him read the first Republican Party platform with the

---

14   G.O.D. and natural law.
15   PragerU, "The Inconvenient Truth about the Democratic Party," YouTube, May 22, 2017.

express purpose of locating the "we love slavery" plank.[16] You *help* while they *do*.

Step 3 will span several years, and just like learning how various fabrics best take their turn in the washing machine, different topics will require different levels of care and attention. Thus, if you want your kids to confidently take on a hostile ideological world armed with refined conservative opinions and responses on difficult topics, they'll need to have had a variety of opportunities to engage the world with your help. They'll need assistance articulating why Jim Crow laws violated rather than validated our founding principles in sixth grade, help with their Three-Fifths Compromise [17] homework in eighth grade, and an editor to look over their "anti-racism is just neo-discrimination" paper sophomore year. In every case, they'll need to *do* the work, but you need to provide varying degrees of *help* in the process.

If you are regularly *helping* your children *do* the challenging work of defending conservative values, they will inevitably start to move on to Step 4: "You do, I watch."

• • •

---

[16]   "Resolved: That the Constitution confers upon Congress sovereign powers over the Territories of the United States for their government; and that in the exercise of this power, it is both the right and the imperative duty of Congress to prohibit in the Territories those twin relics of barbarism—Polygamy, and Slavery," Republican Party Platform, 1856, Digital History/University of Houston.

[17]   PragerU, "Why the 3/5ths Compromise Was Anti-Slavery," YouTube, July 23, 2018.

Katy here.

I remember when my firstborn, McKayla,[18] moved from Step 3 to Step 4 during her sophomore year. She had written a pro-life paper, and I'd helped her find various resources, anticipate objections, and characterize the opposition as charitably as possible. During that time, Georgia passed its heartbeat bill, and her Instagram feed was filled with friends claiming that women would be jailed now that the law had passed. She'd composed a post detailing the actual contents of the bill, debunked a variety of leftist talking points, and had been involved in several back-and-forths. She was risking real-life friendships by defending the right to life of children she would never know without my help. It was only when she texted me a request for "the emanations that form a penumbra's text from Roe V Wade" that I became aware of the battle she'd decided to fight, I realized the time for watching had come. Watch, I did. And cheered.[19]

During Step 4, your kids are, for the most part, standing on their own. You still have a role but, as we detail in chapter 8, not as the *doer* or the *helper*, rather as the *consultant*. You still know more than they do, and certainly have more experience behind enemy lines, so you need to stay connected should they require assistance.

Ideally, by the time kids graduate high school, they regularly dwell in the land of Step 4. You *watch* them from the sidelines as they manage the battles they choose to wage. They are railing about the harms of puberty blockers on social media and writing pro-2A [20]essays without your help.

---

[18] We young Fausts were very avant-garde in naming our firstborn; we thought it was SO original. Turns out McKayla was one of the most popular names for baby girls that year. So much for originality.

[19] And took a sinfully large number of mental parental victory laps.

[20] The second amendment for the uninitiated unwashed masses out there.

Be advised: it is a fantasy to believe that you can skip from Step 1 to Step 4; there is no shortcutting this long road. Step 4 can only begin after your kids have been steeped in Steps 2 and 3, for years, replete with opportunities to grapple with difficult topics safely in your shadow.

· · ·

Stacy here.

The following is a shameless self-congratulatory victory lap.[21] *I knew we were well into the "you do, I watch" phase with our eldest when he asked me to look over the mic-drop letter-bomb he'd penned before he sent it to his overtly political, race-obsessed English literature teacher. This comically Woke teacher treats his captive audience to daily "warm-ups," which exclusively focus on social justice and racism. It's a literature class. Yet, he's nonstop with this garbage every single day. Rowan had finally had enough and wrote:*

> *I read a book one time, named* **Red Scarf Girl.** *It was for this library bingo activity we were doing at my elementary school, and I wasn't really that excited about it because historical fiction isn't really interesting to me. But I had a book bingo board to fill out, so I got to work. Surprisingly, I really liked that book.*
>
> *It told the story of a young Chinese girl experiencing the horrors of Mao's cultural revolution. It was a truly terrifying story; it was unbelievable to me*

---

[21]   And hopefully will give you some hope for the next generation.

that this could happen in real life. Of every event detailed in that book, the "Struggle Session" was the most unnerving. The Communists would seize someone, bring them into a room of their peers, and grill them on account they were suspected of being Bourgeois (a capitalist pig). The accused would be interrogated, psychologically tortured, pressured to confess, and "encouraged" to turn from their "evil ways." An act of contrition, if you will. I enclosed "evil ways" in scare quotes because not everyone they interrogated and tortured was, in fact, a capitalist. Terrifyingly, the bar to get dragged into one of these struggle sessions was as low as a simple accusation. In fact, it was very much like the Salem Witch Trials, as we learned in your class earlier this year. I'm sharing this with you to point out some parallels I've observed.

No one, not one person in this classroom, is racist. No one here hates blacks, Mexicans, Jews, Asians, whites, you name it. No one here endorses, or even has a neutral opinion of, slavery. No one here is OK with segregation of any kind. So, why are we doing this assignment? I suspect it's because you consider yourself more an activist than a teacher and it makes you feel good to be, and teach kids to be, so-called "Anti-racist". Promoting this type of political propaganda means you are one of the "good guys" but in truth, this is exactly what the "good Christians" did in the witch trials, and it is *also the tactic of the Proletariats under Mao. This assignment is a thinly veiled Struggle Session, it's based in fantasy and Boogey Men that simply don't exist in this country any more. Well, it didn't, but you seem to want it to.*

Red Scarf Girl is a lovely, powerful book, and it scares me that people like you, in charge of shaping young minds, are leading us along the exact same paths that those in the book did. This is a path that leads only to destruction, and if you really want to "end racism," I would suggest you simply stop talking about race all the time.

Thanks,
Rowan Manning

Rowan was born fearless, a nonconformist by nature, and that trait comes in handy in an upside-down culture. However, it's not enough to have naturally courageous kids. They have to know what they are *for* so they can reject what they are against. Rowan received a slow-drip of truth throughout his childhood. He also went off half-cocked many times throughout the years with both peers and adults. It's been a bumpy ride, and his mother *might* still panic reflexively when she receives an email from his school, but because he was afforded both teaching and practice, Rowan is going to be an absolute force for good in the world. Your kids can be too.

This slow training handoff begins young. In addition to watching you become an expert on conservatism, your kids should be consuming—whether reading, listening to, or watching—appropriate elementary-age conservative ideas, which we will cover in the next chapter. And we'll offer guidance on what content to filter out of their little worlds. If you ever hope to sit back and "watch" your children successfully fend off the Wokists, you need to start filling them with biological, historical, and economic truth now.

CHAPTER 6

ELEMENTARY SCHOOL—FILTER OUT

If you're still reading, we expect that you're on board with the concepts your children must *conserve*, you understand training supersedes safety in the parenting paradigm, and that you must become an expert because *you* are the training program. At this point, the cultivation of your no-flinch game face is securely fixed, and you know that you must get to your kids first if you have any chance of circumventing Wokist teachers and media influences. You also accept that there's no quick fix, raising conservative kids is a long-road endeavor that entails a slow handoff.

Yet still, the devil is in the details: Is Disney+ OK? What about the playdate invite extended by the classmate with "two moms"? What's the appropriate answer when your eight-year-old asks you about abortion? Do you dodge the question or go into gory details about the difference between chemical and surgical procedures? Or maybe, you wonder if you should come clean and admit that as a stupid teenager *you* had an abortion. How much information is too much, and what amount is too little?

Much of that depends on you and your kiddo. While you do need to answer their questions honestly at this stage, the emphasis during this developmental period is to saturate your kids with truth and beauty,[1] while keeping at bay as much of the false and ugly as possible.

Quoting American evangelist D. L. Moody, "The best way to prove that a stick is crooked is...to lay a straight stick next to it." The elementary school years are *the* years to help your kids whittle their own straight stick on America, faith, marriage, life, race, gender, and economics. It is crucial that they have this stick[2] firmly in hand before they enter middle school. That's because the gloves come OFF in middle school; it is a full-throttle crooked-truths-presented-as-fact environment for which they will need a solid, sturdy stick for self-defense. We intend this chapter to provide general suggestions on what elementary-sized sticks look like. That means *filtering in* truth and beauty while *filtering out* lies and distortions.

---

[1] Highly annoying Christianese phrase Katy has been saying forever. It comes from Plato's "goodness, truth, and beauty" trifecta. When you hear a Jesus fan-clubber say this, they mean "immersed in a Christian/biblical worldview."

[2] Not to be confused with the Ugly Stick.

Leverage the Stages of Learning

"They're little sponges!" exclaims your mother when, much to your shame, she catches your firstborn[3] singing "The Cover of the Rolling Stone" by Dr. Hook, verbatim. As cringy as it might be to listen to your son belt out song lyrics about a freaky old lady with a fondness for ingesting cocaine, there *is* a silver lining in this parenting fail. While exposing your four-year-old to the concept that pills bring thrills might take you out of the running for Parent of the Year, it illustrates the powerful birth to ten years stage of learning.

Classical educators refer to the elementary school years (K-5) as the *grammar* stage. The grammar—read *rules*—stage, a.k.a. the "little sponge stage," focuses on memorization. Classical educators spend these years filling their kids' minds with facts such as multiplication tables, Latin vocabulary, geography, historical figures, and anatomy. In essence, this approach takes advantage of a child's ability to unquestioningly absorb information and builds a factual foundation for each subject from which they will draw as their education becomes more complex and nuanced.

Middle school is characterized by the *logic* phase. During this period students are encouraged to think logically, independently, and critically as they begin to develop an ability to defend their point of view. They're tasked with the re-exploration of the information gathered during their grammar phase and to test it against reality.[4] The logic phase is focused

---

[3] Stacy's firstborn, and to be clear, "Cover of the Rolling Stone" is a harmless family singalong, Karen.
[4] "Lived experience" for you lefties.

on investigating the *whys* behind the information memorized during their sponge phase. The best practices for responding to your middle schoolers' inevitable skepticism toward the facts compiled throughout the grammar stage are covered in chapter 7.

The debate, rather, *rhetoric*, phase commences in high school. Teens understand what they believe, they are aware of the standard cultural push-back to those beliefs, and they're refining their ability to articulate their thoughts independently. Thus, when it comes to confronting contentious cultural issues, the emergence of the debater can be met with parental step-back as your responsibilities morph from teacher to consultant. This is the final phase of the slow hand-off, the "*you do, I watch*" stage. Chapter 8 offers some helpful[5] strategies on how to stay connected to your high schooler as you enjoy your promotion to the role of consultant.

The classical education model is very similar to the slow handoff we described in chapter 5. In this chapter we'll highlight aspects of the sponge phase that should help you discern what, when, and how to expose your kids to right-thinking truth.

Elementary School

During the elementary school years, kids are wired to unquestioningly absorb information, but they're not yet capable of filtering out falsehoods, debating dubious claims, or

---

5   We hope.

understanding whether they're being exposed to inappropriate material. That's why it's imperative that, as much as possible, this phase is free of distorted depictions of sex, gender, violence, history, and competing worldviews, whether from media or agenda-driven adults. Developmentally they require an external filter, and that filter is you.

The power adults have over the formation of a child's pliable mind in this phase cannot be understated, which is precisely why the Wokists went berserk over Florida's Parental Rights in Education Act.[6] This legislation simply restricts teachers from introducing sex and gender content to the under-third-grade crowd, but because Woke activist educators know how susceptible children are to indoctrination in the grammar/sponge phase, they went into a full meltdown over the new law. Get thyself[7] woke to this critical stage and use this precious time to indoctrinate your children yourself.

The main feature of the grammar/sponge phase is minimal resistance. At this age, kids generally accept the information imparted by adults whom they like and trust without question. It's the optimal season for a firehose of truth and beauty.[8] This is the ideal phase to help your children construct a right-thinking worldview curated by the two adults they like and trust the most—Mom and Dad.

Just as the classically educated kids memorize the facts of each discipline, conservative grammar-phase training emphasizes facts—that is, the truth and beauty[9] that undergirds

---

[6]   The so-called "Don't Say Gay" bill.
[7]   Stacy's new preferred pronouns are thy/thyself.
[8]   So. Annoying. I could remove it, but it's more fun to harass her publicly.
[9]   HONESTLY.

conservative thinking. Through age ten, your most important job is to teach and model the good and immutable realities of the world around them.

Below we outlined some ways to introduce the "What Is Conservatism?" principles to your little sponges:

. . .

On the nature of America. Read and reread the Constitution and the Declaration of Independence.[10] Learn about the lives of American founding fathers; the Rush Revere book series is an excellent, engaging resource for young readers to sponge up the truth of our founding. Introduce great American women like Susan B. Anthony and Amelia Earhart, and inspiring Americans such as Frederick Douglass, Harriet Tubman, and George Washington Carver; the Heroes of Liberty books are all the rage with conservative parents of kids aged seven–twelve. Use original sources, not commentary, when researching US history. Watch documentaries about the heroes that made the ultimate sacrifice to protect our way of life. Documentaries bring people to life in a way that bridges the span of time; viewing these men and women as real people helps make the consequences of their actions more impactful. Attend a naturalization ceremony; helping to welcome freshly minted Americans into the fold is an easily manufactured object lesson in watching people from all cultures come together under an *idea*.[11] Never miss an opportunity to point out examples

---

[10] One of the most eloquently written F-yous of all time.

[11] *E pluribus unum*, out of many, one; the motto of the United States.

where the un-American concept of "equity" (equal outcome) has replaced the very American ideal of "equality" (equal opportunity).

Honest depictions of the ugly chapters of US history are also essential to include in the curriculum of truth-teaching parents. Read *Roll of Thunder, Hear My Cry* together. Explain the horrors of the Trail of Tears, and make movie night *Hidden Figures.*

Encourage patriotism in your young conservatives, despite our nation's past failures. Teach them to not only *pledge* allegiance but also *feel* an allegiance to this specific country, its ideas, and its history. Reinforce that they are citizens of *this* land, and that's something to be proud of.

Filter out sources that focus on America's sins at the exclusion of her achievements. Anything that identifies itself with "diversity, equity, and inclusion" is the plague; treat it accordingly. Scrub your home of the scourge that is NPR[12]. NPR is one of the most prolific purveyors of the Woke worldview; if you believe they really consider all things in their *All Things Considered* program, you probably also believe FOX News' claim that they're "fair and balanced." Neither is true. Disney is out-and-proud about their intent to infuse their content with as much of the LGBT+ agenda as possible; filter them out. Favor *VeggieTales* over *SpongeBob.*

Filter out messages that encourage "global citizenship." We should, of course, be concerned for the well-being of all peoples, especially those who are suffering. But we have a

---

[12] National Public Radio, or more honestly Next up Probably Racism.

special allegiance to, and should prioritize, the protection and prosperity of Americans.

. . .

Religion/freedom of conscience. Saturate your child in God, memorize scripture together, sing hymns[13] to them at bedtime. Be a presence at church; teach by example how to be generous with fellow believers and serve the community. Show them how "being in, but not of, the world[14]" manifests; confess and forgive one another's trespasses and be faithful in good times and bad. Point out hospitals named after saints in your town as examples of faith-based works. Seek out and unify with Muslim parents[15] in the fight against groomers on your school board when they push innocence-stealing sex-ed curriculum.

Filter out anything masquerading as "Christian" including "churches" flying the rainbow flag[16] as wolves in sheep's clothing that flagrantly celebrate sin with the co-opted symbol of God's promise. Scrutinize Sunday school curriculum, vacation

---

[13]   Hymns are rhyming orthodoxy for you sinful, unchurched types.

[14]   More Christian speak. Jesus instructs His followers to be "in, and not of, the world," which means His fan club is supposed to attract nonbelievers because they live among others but live differently than others. This in-not-of is the best way to introduce others to the faith because it's not preachy, it's simply lived. Katy kills this. Stacy? Work in progress.

[15]   Our district carefully translates school announcements into numerous languages. Yet LGBTQ events, notices advising that IUDs can be obtained at the school clinic and policy changes related to locker and bathrooms don't tend to reach immigrant families, especially Muslim parents who (the district knows) would be properly horrified. Befriend these moms and dads—they could use your help navigating the Woke landscape.

[16]   It's only a matter of time before these faux-churches will be celebrating gluttony by hosting fat-pride events.

bible school lessons, and the "What We Believe" statement of your kid's Christian school.

. . .

On the nature of man and woman. From the moment they utter mama[17] and dada, observe and celebrate the difference between men and women. Decouple these conversations from superficial stereotypes, such as women like to cook, men do yard work, and instead emphasize the glorious biological differences between the sexes. Talk with your kids regularly about the gratitude you feel for their father's willingness to work hard so that you can stay home with them. Marvel aloud at the fact your wife's body makes the perfect food for the new baby. Drive home that our bodies are not obstacles to our true selves, but that they *are* our true selves.

Filter out gender ideology. Absolutely refuse the normalization of the idea that it's acceptable to mutilate the body to conform to a gender-confused mind.[18] You'll find this poisonous message everywhere in children's content quietly cloaked in a trans-species package. Whether the double-mastectomy-scarred transgender beaver in *Blue's Clues*, or in *Lulu Is a Rhinoceros*, a book about a bulldog who believes she is a rhino. Instead, make your bedtime story *Johnny the Walrus* by Matt Walsh.[19]

. . .

---

[17] Or apple. Ya, apple. Rowan has always been a special snowflake.
[18] No liposuction for the anorexic, no puberty blockers for the gender-confused.
[19] If you're not a member of Matt's Sweet Baby Gang, you should avail yourself of all things Matt Walsh posthaste.

On the nature of marriage. Hopefully you are doing this parenting gig while in a loving, supportive marriage. If so, you can never make too much of the God-given object lesson playing out daily in your home. There are four norms that define a marriage: monogamy, complementarity, permanence, and exclusivity.[20] Name and explain each of them in a variety of age-appropriate ways as your children mature.

- "Marriage is mono-gamous; 'mono' means one and 'gamy' is marriage. I'm only married to one person, your daddy."
- "It takes a man and woman to make a baby; that's why it takes a man and woman to be in a marriage, because kids need both their mom and dad. In fact, kids have always been the reason for marriage."
- "Kids deserve to have a lifelong relationship with their mom and dad—not just when they're two months, or two years, or twelve years old. That's why the promise of marriage includes 'till death do us part.'"
- "I save my kisses for your daddy alone."

If you find yourself without a faithful husband or wife with you on this parenting journey, our hearts go out to you. This is not our first time at the rodeo so we know many of you single parents are not single by choice. Whatever the reason your spouse refused to do the heavy lifting of vow-keeping or

---

[20] If you're looking for a heady exploration on this topic, we'd suggest *What Is Marriage?* by Sherif Girgis, Ryan T. Anderson, and Robert T. George (New York: Encounter Books, 2012). If, however, we're more your intellectual speed, check our first book, *Them Before Us*. Also? We're funnier.

child-rearing, we're sorry you didn't get the commitment you and your kiddos deserved. Raising conservative kids is challenging enough when both parents live in the same home and speak the same language. The task when co-parenting, or harder still, war-parenting with a hostile ex becomes more difficult by magnitudes.

For you doubly taxed single parents, whether you've suffered the death of your spouse, the end of your marriage, or got pregnant out of wedlock, it is important to identify a trustworthy couple with whom your child is close and talk about what a great example they are of a healthy marriage during the grammar phase.[21] Perhaps lifetimers like Oma and Opa would fit the bill, or maybe your BFF has an enviable marriage to look to as an example. Highlight the ways that such a couple fulfills the norms of marriage and encourage them to talk with your child about the hard-but-good realities of a lifelong commitment.

Filter out messaging that glamorizes any form of nonmarital sex, normalizes hookups, features homosexual relationships, or depicts graphic sex, extramarital affairs, gay parents, or poly unions.[22] If the two moms your daughter's classmate explicitly promote the false equivalence of marriage and gay marriage, filter them out. If these two women are respectful of

---

[21] Between our two families, the total number of parents that hail from intact families is zero. Despite the brokenness of our own childhood homes, we all knew what kind of family we wanted to cultivate as adults largely because, as children, we had examples of healthy marriages. No child is doomed, but those in broken homes need to be shown that a well-functioning family is possible.

[22] Watch out for *The Family Book*; that literary garbage will have your kid believing the difference between having two moms is as inconsequential as a family's preference for Chinese takeout vs. pizza.

your convictions and don't overtly seek to influence your child, you've got a great opportunity to model what "in the world not of the world" looks like for her in real time by building a relationship with them.

. . .

On the nature of the parent-child relationship. You and your kids have a unique bond exclusive of any other humans on the planet. You wouldn't have been satisfied leaving the hospital with just any baby; you wanted to leave with yours, obviously, because you have a right to your child. Likewise, your children have a right to be raised by their mom and dad.[23]

You cement this parent-child bond acting as their primary educator. Done well, it subversively teaches your child how a parent should behave. This training is ubiquitous; it happens during the mundane minutiae of day-to-day life.

Reinforce the fact that parents are responsible for giving children what they need because they have the greatest investment in their child's future.

Filter out, if possible, any programs or adults that condition your child to depend on them, not you, for their basic needs.

. . .

---

[23] If you have adopted children, in addition to telling them that they belong with you forever, teach them that they had a right to be adopted, but you did not have a right to adopt them. *You* were not owed children; *they* were owed parents who underwent a lengthy process to prove themselves worthy.

Katy here:

One lovely summer afternoon my brood and I were at the park with Stacy and company. Lunchtime rolled around and the tax-dollar-funded "Free Summer Lunch" wagon pulled into the parking lot and began distributing sack lunches. Not missing a beat, my kids were first in line for their share of junk masquerading as food. Stacy, however, to my immediate shame, looking into her children's "can we?" eyes answered, "Those are not for you. Your parents provide for your needs, not the state. Here's your lunch."

It pains me to say, because she won't ever let me live it down,[24] *but Stacy's conservative parenting was an embarrassment of riches in teaching that day. And as difficult as it is to regale you with her superior showing, especially when compared to my lackluster performance, she'd provided the pitch-perfect example of how to drive home the point that children belong to their parents, not to the state.*

• • •

On the right to life. Passionately make the case for the dignity of all human life, at both its fragile beginning and frail end. People of all ages, all races, and all ability levels deserve to have their right to life legally protected—which is the most important function of government. Have a running dialogue about the Bill of Rights and explain that none of the other rights matter unless the right to life is protected. Watch Live Action's *Meet Baby Olivia* and marvel at the miracle of life. When a pregnancy occurs in your orbit, narrate its course to your littles. Babysit your toddler niece together and pay visits

---

[24] She already has.

to your bedridden great-grandma and ask that she treat you to tales of her post-Depression childhood. Vulnerable people—both children and the elderly—need special care, and the people best suited to provide that care is family.

Unfortunately, not everyone believes that humans have an inherent dignity or the right to life. So, in the grammar phase, when your children ask, you will need to provide honest, simple answers to difficult questions about abortion, or when Uncle Ed champions "death with dignity," or why they notice there doesn't seem to be any people with Down syndrome under the age of thirty.

Filter out books that elevate animals to the status of human. We cherish and care for animals, but they don't have the same rights people do.[25] *Filter out* your pro-choice college roommate who casually (read: purposefully) drops euphemisms like "reproductive health" and "birthing persons" when your kids are within earshot.

. . .

On the matter of race. Most importantly,[26] teach them that true diversity is measured by the diversity of thoughts and ideas, and that using skin color as a measure of diversity is racist and insulting. When you see an interracial couple, comment on how sweet it is that he pulled out the chair for her. Your kids will learn that race doesn't matter, character does.

---

[25] When the crazy cat-lady neighbor prattles on about her fur babies, ask your child if it would be considered child abuse if you fed him from a bowl on the floor or locked him in a kennel eight hours a day.

[26] Most MOST importantly, just don't be a racist douchebag.

Venerate black Americans who've overcome humble beginnings like Condoleezza Rice, Clarence Thomas, and Ben Carson. Study the life of immigrant patriots and their children, including Enes Kanter Freedom and Nikki Haley.

Filter out: Antiracist Baby by Ibram X. Kendi[27] and other racist propaganda that tells children that they are either oppressors or oppressed because of their skin color.

• • •

On economics. The principle of the free market—that is, to barter and trade items of value and to receive a reward for your work—is the most organic system of human exchange. These concepts can and should be taught early; you can use the immediate cash reward of a classic lemonade stand, make the wages of tedious weed-pulling a double-decker ice cream cone, or, after a summer spent mowing lawns, let your kid decide whether the Lego Death Star is *actually* worth a thousand bucks when he's spending his own money. Help them learn the tangible way that work is rewarded.

Talk about your work or your husband's work. Explain that Daddy worked late for overtime pay, that more time away from his family is a sacrifice but provides more money, because nothing is free. Model good economics in your mini-society—only buying what your family can afford now and then explaining that macro-societies should operate under the same principles. Pay in cash. Explain that birthday presents are sweet, but they are *gifts* not entitlements. When you do see

---

[27] Race hustler that rivals the likes of Rev. Jesse Jackson and Rev. Al Sharpton.

a kid who is unhappy because he didn't get the *Japanese* version of the Pokémon card he wanted, help your child recognize that entitlement is ugly on an individual level and devastating if an entire society is infected with an entitlement mentality.

Explain that money functions as a storage device of our labor and life energy, that it's the physical representation of the time we must spend away from our family in order to provide. Connect this concept to the evils of theft; that is, a thief is not just stealing things, they are taking something that cannot be replaced—they are stealing Mommy and Daddy's time.

Filter out the urge to lean on material goods as a substitute for relationship and connection. It's OK—no, it's good—for little kids to hear the words "we can't afford it," or better still, "we won't afford it" when it comes to frivolous purchases.

• • •

In the subjects above, we've recommended that you "filter out" certain people during the grammar phase. We are not suggesting that you cut off people with whom you disagree, only that you draw a line with those who seek to evangelize your children into their progressive worldview. If you're unable to keep them from exposure to Woke disciples, a conversation is in order. Something like, "Hey, you and I disagree about all these things—abortion, religion, removing that statue of Teddy Roosevelt, climate change, gay marriage, racist cops—but I don't want you to talk with my kids about them. When they are older and more capable of engaging with your ideas, you're welcome to have a conversation with them. But for now,

let's keep things apolitical." If they respect that request, great!
If they don't? Filter. Them. Out.

The World Is Your Classroom

The world is your classroom, and you are the teacher. Lucky
for you, reality reflects the accuracy of conservatism. You need
not plan instructional conversations with your littles; daily life
presents myriad opportunities to indoctrinate your children
into truth and beauty.[28] Your curriculum is dependent on your
becoming hyperaware of the opportunities for illustrating
right-thinking that present themselves throughout the day. It's
biblical, really.[29]

Wokists understand the value of weaving sex and gender theory into every subject from literature classes to math
classes, and most often social studies classes. You need to be
just as, if not more, deliberate about weaving worldview teaching into everyday things. Be on the lookout daily for instances
where you can draw a connection to biological, economic, and
historical reality. Your kiddo wins a soccer game? Talk about
why merit matters. See a dad tossing his baby in the air? Talk
about the wonderful differences between moms and dads.
Walking behind an immigrant family? Discuss the ways our
founding principles make this country such a desirable destination for immigrants. Swearing under your breath at the gas

---

[28]   Lord help us, Katy just can't help her Christianese ways.
[29]   The Author of all authors puts it this way, "Teach [the truth] diligently to your
children...when you sit in your house, and when you walk by the way, and when
you lie down, and when you rise."

pump? Play a Milton Friedman lecture[30] on economics during the drive home. In short, every moment of wonder or beauty or instance of injustice is a teaching opportunity. Capitalize on them, ya capitalist.

The grammar phase also involves answering their every-day questions with *brief, honest, age-appropriate* answers. Here are some ideas to get your brain churning; it's best to have put some thought into your response to the crazy crap that will assuredly be rattling about in your kid's head when they arrive home from The World.

- Your kid comes home and reports that today's carpet time story was about a girl with two daddies. *Nobody has two daddies. Some kids are parented by two men, that's true, but everyone has exactly one mom and one dad. The phrase "two daddies" means she isn't being raised by her mommy and every child needs, wants, and deserves their mommy.*

- At tuck-up time your daughter asks if you can just take a pill and not be pregnant anymore. *That's true. Unfortunately, humans have devised all kinds of ways to kill their unborn children. Babies need us to speak up and defend their right to life.*

- Your kid asks for help memorizing the Land Acknow-ledgment handed out in class today. *Did your teacher happen to mention which tribe they took the land from? And what about tribes before them? Native Americans were composed of many fierce cultures and were overwhelmed*

---

[30] Friedman's appearances on *The Phil Donahue Show* are particularly delicious.

> *by a changing world, guns, and an influx of people. The
> same thing has happened in all cultures all over the world
> from the beginning of time. It's in the nature of human
> beings. Tribal leaders signed treaties to end disputes; that's
> politics, not theft.*

- Your son asks why his friend's dad dropped him off at
  school wearing a dress and high heels today. *A man can
  put on a dress, but that doesn't make him a woman. Your
  body makes you a male or female, not what you wear.*

- Your daughter asks you if you ever had an abortion.
  *I'm ashamed to admit I did. I was young and dumb, and
  I didn't have the guidance from my mom you have from
  me. My ignorance cost you an older sibling, and I mourn
  my terrible decision all the time. I believed the world's lies
  about teen pregnancy ruining my life. But now that I've
  learned how wonderful children are by getting to be your
  mom? I regret it even more. I think if I'd had the baby, it
  would have made me a better person. Because that's what
  parenthood does, but no one told me the truth.*

In this primary, spongey, foundational phase of learning,
make sure you maximize your kids' exposure to truth and
beauty.[31] Illustrate the goodness of core conservative principles throughout their day and by leveraging the world around
them. The window for them to sponge up your instruction

---

[31]   JESUS TAKE THE WHEEL.

doesn't last long, and you need them to understand what they are *for*, so in middle school you can teach them to deploy their straight stick to identify for themselves ideas they must stand *against*.

<————————————————>

CHAPTER 7

MIDDLE SCHOOL—BUILD THEIR FILTER

*K*aty *here.*

"You don't believe that gay marriage should be legal?" All eyes around the lunch table were suddenly trained on sixth-grade McKayla. "So that means you hate gay people!" exclaimed her Woke classmate.

"No, it doesn't," McKayla replied. "My grandma is gay, and I love her. So, what is your argument?"

"Well, if a man and a woman who love each other can get married, then two men who love each other should be able to get married, and two women who love each other should be able to get married. There's no difference."

"The difference is that a man and a woman make a baby," McKayla bravely countered. "Two men can't make a baby together, and neither can two women."

"Oh, I guess that's true. But the two men or the two women could just adopt if they wanted a baby."

"Yes, but adoption is not about giving kids to adults. Adoption is about finding homes for children who don't have parents, and all children need moms and dads," insisted McKayla.

"Well, I think kids just need adults who love them," responded the budding Wokist.

"No," countered McKayla, "dads teach kids certain lessons, moms teach kids other lessons, and kids need both kinds of lessons."

Amazingly, McKayla was able to communicate three truths about marriage and family that escape most adults: (1) she understood that the purpose of marriage is not about adult feelings, it's about children, (2) that no adult has a right to a child, and (3) the important distinct and complementary benefits men and women bring to child-rearing. Further, because she had watched her mother fiercely love and maintain a healthy relationship with her grandmother, the accusation of "hating" gay people was easily dismissed.

I remember thinking ICANTBELIEVEITACTUALLYWORKED as she entertained me with her lunch-time drama on our walk home.

After a relatively sheltered Christian elementary education, my husband and I spent the summer preparing[1] our firstborn to enter public school. Not just any public school, mind you. We were sending her into a lion's den—her new school is a crown jewel of the Seattle school district, a loud and proud Woke school that emphasizes "social justice," which, at the time, mainly translated to the promotion of gay "rights." Thus, McKayla was subjected to a 2.5-month firehose of parental prepping on everything from abortion to

---

[1]   Crash coursing.

same-sex attraction to Marxism to transgenderism to marriage. It wasn't pretty, and it's frankly a miracle that she did not suffer an eye sprain from all the eye rolling. She'd plead, "Do we have to do this again? I'd answer, "Yes because I want you to know more than anyone else."

And know more she did. *Not only did she retain core concepts like "dads and moms offer distinct and complementary benefits to children," but she'd capably translated this truth into the sixth-grade lexicon. "Dads teach kids certain lessons; moms teach kids different lessons. And kids need both kinds." It proved to me that middle schoolers not only can handle these big conversations, they can replicate them.*

Build Their Filter

During middle school, your training tactic needs to shift from filtering out Woke ideas on their behalf to constructing their own internal filter, built to recognize and debunk Woke ideas out in the wild. You helped them whittle their straight stick in the early years; this is the season to introduce and analyze the degree of crookedness in the Woke sticks they'll encounter in middle school.

Around age ten to twelve kids enter the critical-thinking "logic" phase of learning. A good indication that this developmental shift has taken place is the pushback you start to get from your tween, often in the form of, "How can we be sure that's true?" or "But what if you're wrong?" It's natural for parents to be caught off guard when their kids begin challenging core conservative concepts that, only a month prior, they were happily regurgitating.

But fear not, these questions don't mean your son or daughter is rejecting your worldview. It's actually evidence that they're ready for higher-level information. The time has come to introduce them to the opposition's take on cultural issues. We cannot stress enough how important it is that every conservative kid takes on culture war issues that arise in the hellish middle school years armed with more ~~ammunition~~[2] information than their peers. Middle school kids who fancy themselves as Woke are heady with the power of groupthink, high on belonging to the in-crowd, and just as cruel as they've always been at that age; worse still, these days, the toxic pubescent cocktail that is middle school has been overrun by Woke adult allies dressed in teachers' clothing.

The Left will introduce culture war topics in ways that distort the truth and destroy your children's innocence, whether through the pro-choice walkout or the valorization of Che Guevara.[3] You need to explain Woke ideas in a way that keeps your child's innocence intact while also teaching them to walk softly with their big conservative stick.

Values to conserve: *The Middle School Edition.*

· · ·

---

[2] According to the Manning children, school shooter jokes are all the rage amongst the high school crowd, and Stacy's sense of humor never developed past that of a freshman.

[3] That murderous Marxist dirtbag was finally captured on the run with an unfired rifle, begging for his life and claiming he was "worth more to the Americans alive."

On the nature of America. Keep the concept of individual rights in the foreground and emphasize how truly revolutionary the concept of a government based on *equal opportunity for all* was in 1776. Stress that society in pursuit of *equal outcomes for all* does not result in everyone *succeeding* equally, but that equal opportunity means everyone has the ability to improve their status. Explain that forced "equality" can only result in everyone *suffering* equally. In socialist states very few can be a CEO, but everyone *can* live in poverty and be a slave to the state. Remind them regularly that this great country was founded upon individual liberty; that we each have the freedom to pursue what makes us happy, which does not and could never translate to equal outcomes; that no one is guaranteed success in this life but freedom affords both success and failure because it honors a person's ability to choose.

As we see it, there are two major threats to the American way of life: one external, the other internal.

The external threat comes in the form of globalists. Powerful bureaucrats and heads of major global corporations[4] fancy themselves capable of top-down control; they speak of the "great reset" needed to usher in the "new world order," a two-tiered system in which the elites will control the masses with a one-world government. We will no longer be American citizens but citizens of the world. You can see this desire for global domination expressed in their economy-be-damned climate agenda[5] or the World Health Organization's[6] use of

---

[4] See supervillain George Soros and his number two, Klaus Schwab.
[5] Google "Dutch farmer fertilizer protests."
[6] Basically a puppet org of the Chinese Communist Party.

COVID-19 as a tool to consolidate power. Like all progressive ideas, being a "global citizen" sounds nice. But in practice it concentrates power in the hands of a few and diminishes the autonomy of the individual and the nation.

Highlight nations that are reclaiming sovereignty from global powers. The Hungarians, for example, are reviving a spirit of pride in their own, unique, historical traditions and language, much to the ire of their European Union overlords.[7] The Italians elected a conservative prime minister passionate about the importance of family values and gender roles, who also believes Italy, instead of Brussels, should determine what is best for Italy. Japan is reconstituting its military to defend its own borders against an increasingly aggressive China. The takeaway: it's good for a nation to see to its own best interests and the well-being of its own citizens; borders and nationalism make the world a safer place.

The biggest *internal* threat comes courtesy of Marxist-based critical theory. Critical theory is a force of destruction to whatever system, institution, or tradition to which it is applied. The opening act for the critical theorist is to conjure a utopian version of whatever "next thing"[8] has their panties in a bunch. Next up, they critique whatever current cultural structure[9] they've got in their sights by railing against all the ways

---

[7] Bullies.

[8] These types of people are protest junkies. Their lives lack meaning, and the rush they feel after getting their rage on doesn't last; they will never be sated. "Permanent revolution," Marx called it.

[9] Critical feminist theory maintains that all men are oppressors and all women are oppressed. Critical queer theory asserts that heterosexuals are oppressors and anyone who belongs to the alphabet mafia is oppressed. And critical race theory views all whites as oppressors and all minorities are oppressed.

in which it falls short of their utopian fantasy. The final act features a cast of riled-up, ignorant student-types, passionate but misguided by these so-called intellectuals who set about destroying that system,[10] to make way for the emergence of the fantastical utopian vision imagineered by the critical theorist.

Critical race theory (CRT) is particularly important for your kids to understand because it is a power player in the deconstruction of traditional American values. It's profoundly un-American and unjust because it categorizes people by their group identity, not their individuality. For example, CRT is responsible for the phrase "white privilege" and views a dirt-poor, uneducated white man who barely escaped his meth-addicted single mom as equally privileged as a well-educated white man from an intact family born with a silver spoon in his mouth, simply because of their shared skin color. Examples abound among a variety of intersectional[11] groups. Critical theory divides people according to oppressors and the oppressed, with the former perpetually guilty and the latter incapable of sin.

CRT is everywhere, and it's kind of like getting a new car, the kind you never saw on the road before but now that you own one, you spot them daily. Once you notice CRT, you'll start seeing it in everything.

· · ·

---

[10] A.k.a. activism.

[11] Social categorizations such as race, class, and gender as they apply to a given individual or group, regarded as creating overlapping and interdependent systems of discrimination or disadvantage.

Stacy here.

After one particularly cringy episode between Rowan and a clan of Woke middle school peers, followed by an epic No-Flinch failure on my part, I found myself on the phone with his principal. This gentleman, a black American who attended college on a chess scholarship, obviously a man possessing a high intellect, was calling me after hours from the ferry he takes to his home on Bainbridge Island. Bainbridge happens to be one of the more exclusive, well-heeled zip codes in our region. It's no surprise he did so well for himself; as a principal in our district he is surely a member of the six-figure club.

The area code displayed on my phone made his Woke programming and apparent blindness to it all the more shocking as he explained to me that "only white people can be racist, blacks can be prejudiced, not racist, because of the power/privilege structure."

Said the black principal headed to his home on an island where the median home price is one million bucks, twice that of the district in which he is employed, a price point that very few district families, of any color, could afford.

Suffice to say, I was speechless.

Putting it mildly, the Woke are BIG FANS of CRT; division, otherizing, and identity via group-labeling are very effective tools to wield in power retention. The irony of this flawed Woke theory should be obvious from history and current-day atrocities. Explain to your middle schooler that group-identification is at the root of the greatest injustices of the world, including America's failures. The Jews were dehumanized during the Holocaust, the pre-born dehumanized in the abortion debate,

and blacks were enslaved because they were seen not as individuals but as one subhuman group. Driving home the importance of seeing people as individuals with unique life experiences and God-given rights is the best remedy for injustice,
not the cause of it.

• • •

Religion/freedom of conscience. When your kids ask if Jesus
really is the only way to heaven, go on an apologetic expedi-
tion and compare the claims of the five major religions[12] of
the world, including the West's default religion of secular
humanism, together. Familiarize yourselves with textual crit-
icism and marvel that when compared to other ancient texts,
the New Testament outscores, in both number of manuscripts
and reliability, every other ancient text. If you do have a kid
questioning the veracity of the bible, making this discovery
together can go a long way to instill biblical confidence, and
surely get you a lot further than "the bible says it, I believe it,
that settles it."[13]

The importance of freedom of religion cannot be understated.[14] Protected by the First Amendment, religion is collo-
quially referred to as our "first freedom" as it literally holds
pole position[15] on the list of things for which "Congress shall

---

[12]   For the lazy out there, they are Hinduism, Judaism, Buddhism, Christianity,
     and Islam.
[13]   A phrase that adequately captures the authority and supremacy of scripture, but
     holy/wholly inadequate as a training tactic.
[14]   For a terrifying nexus of identifying people by their group identity and forbidding
     freedom of religion, type "Uyghur" into the Google.
[15]   Stacy's yahoo daddy WAS a race car driver after all. You can take the girl out of
     the pits...

make no law." A government that can limit religious freedoms can limit free thought and free expression. The right to free expression of religion must be defended regardless of which beliefs, religion, faith, or creed is threatened. Explain to your kids that religious minorities are often most in need of constitutional protections; e.g., while Jews make up only 2.4 percent of the US population, they are the target of nearly 60 percent of hate crimes. Study the persecutions of Barronelle Stutzman and Jack Phillips, two American Christians in the legal crosshairs of the alphabet mafia because they want to run their private business guided by their Christian principles, to see an illustration of the direct relationship between free expression and the right to live in accordance with religious beliefs.

While freedom of speech does protect the right of people to say wretched things, it is paramount in protecting unpopular, minority positions.[16] Do a thought experiment with your kids: have them think of an example of cancellation or social media ban that occurred because someone said something popular with the in-crowd.[17] The function of curtailing speech is the consolidation of power. Wokists want the power to throttle religious and conscience freedoms, and they're doing it under the guise of "safety." Watch for and point out the many occurrences in daily life that, because it makes someone else uncomfortable, someone's speech is referred to as "hateful" or even "violent."[18] Phrases such as "men cannot become women"

---

[16] No one is clamoring for the censorship of "Happy Birthday" or "No, your butt looks fantastic in those jeans."

[17] This is a fool's errand. The tech overlords bans are a one-way street, headed right.

[18] Except for the times when "silence is violence," of course. Keeping everything straight, dear reader?

or "kids need moms and dads" are enough for the Woke to light their torches and clamor for your cancellation. Protecting the first freedom is our greatest ally in the fight against tyranny—rinse and repeat.[19]

• • •

On the nature of man and woman. Do your homework on gender dysphoria; it's a real mental illness, and those who suffer from it deserve our compassion, not ridicule.[20] Learn about social contagions to understand the phenomena largely responsible for the massive increase in trans-identifying[21] youth. Read commentary on the discontinuation of sex-reassignment surgery at Johns Hopkins University by the pioneer of the procedure, Dr. Paul McHugh, in which he concluded, "Transgendered men do not become women, nor do transgendered women become men." He continued, "All become feminized men or masculinized women."

If your kiddo didn't already suffer through it during carpet story time in third grade, read *I Am Jazz* by Jazz Jennings, then watch some clips of Jazz's long-running reality show, and follow that up with recent headlines that reveal his[22] many complications from the numerous "bottom surgeries" he's endured and the one hundred-plus pounds he's packed on as a result of the artificial estrogen they've pumped through his body. Google

---

[19] A little laundry lingo for you call-back lovers.
[20] Those who are profiting from transgender "treatment"? Ridicule away. Better? Imprison them, because what they are doing to children is criminal.
[21] I hate myself for typing in Woke lingo. Abhor, despise, and detest.
[22] Yes, his.

"de-transitioners" and read the myriad stories of woe and regret, of so-called vulvas made with colons that smell of feces. These are stories you'll need to vet before you share them with your tweens; they are not written with the faint of heart in mind. Discuss the suspect ethics of Big Pharma and the cosmetic surgeons who prey on gender-confused children and their families for profit, regardless of the social contagion currently spreading or the glaring co-morbidities with which they have presented.

Research swimmer William Thomas, formerly ranked 554th men's freestyle swimmer for Penn State, who's now competing as "Lia" Thomas, which makes him the top-ranked "female" swimmer because he's a man. A man that "came out"[23] as a trans woman, which is a man. Google the ridiculous images of this guy towering over the female swimmers from whom he's stealing titles. Read the testimonials from his[24] brave teammates who've spoken about their discomfort with the league's expectation that they should be fine getting nude in the locker room around a man who says he's a woman and their fear of being labeled a transphobe if they give voice to their discomfort. The major lesson for middle schoolers: when it comes to sports, prisons,[25] shelters, bathrooms, and dressing rooms blurring the line between male and female victimizes women 100 percent of the time.

. . .

---

[23] He, with his ridiculously conspicuous penis bulging in his one-piece swimsuit, says he feels a thing, so the college swim world is reordered. Because William feels.

[24] Yes, his. Him. That dude.

[25] Women are getting pregnant—that is, being raped—in all-female prisons thanks to violent men who "identify" as women.

On the nature of marriage. Your tween needs to know the myriad ways adults are arranging their romantic lives these days. This includes shacking up, hooking up, gay marriage, open marriage, polygamy,[26] and sologamy.[27] Focus on how these diverse arrangements all have one thing in common: they exclude a child's mother or father and/or put children at an increased risk of abuse and neglect. At this age tweens are ready for the information in our first book, *Them Before Us: Why We Need a Global Children's Rights Movement*. In it, we analyze all of these "modern" adult assemblages viewed through the lens of hard data, personalized by the real-life narratives of children who've grown up in these environments. Spoiler alert, there is only one family formula that consistently results in the best outcome for children, and that is the safety and security of lifelong, dual-sex marriage.[28]

• • •

On the nature of the parent-child relationship. Follow up on your conversation about modern families and the harm they inflict on children when they are intentionally denied a relationship with their mother or father, with what happens when a tyrannical state usurps the role of parents. Explore how Marxist regimes of the past exploited children to forward their quest for control by researching the Hitler Youth and Mao's Red Guard. Read *Red Scarf Girl* together. Talk about why the traditional family is the enemy of socialism, which teaches that

---

[26] Throuple is a thing. God help us.

[27] Likely more post-publishing date as the social breakdown continues apace.

[28] And no statistical case can be made to the contrary.

if children cannot rely on their parents, the government must step in. By providing the support their children need, parents preclude them from turning to government for guidance.

Today, it's more than just the government seeking to drive a wedge between parents and children. Look for examples in media and academia that promote an anti-parent message. Watch out for the school counselor who derides your faith, and alert your children to trans-activist organizations designed to "help" children run away from their parents and arrange for them to be placed with new "queer-friendly" guardians.[29] Explain to your tween that the family unit is under assault because it's the primary institution that stifles government overreach. Strong personal bonds, especially familial bonds, most especially the parent and child bond, represent the greatest threat to Woke dominion.

• • •

On the right to life. Revisit the science of fetal development you covered in elementary school and reinforce the fact that a new, distinct human life is formed at the moment of conception. Depending on your child's level of sensitivity, explain abortion procedures in detail. They'll rightly recoil in horror upon seeing images of aborted children, which is probably the most effective pro-life argument of all. They'll learn that if you cannot stand to look at a thing, we shouldn't be doing that thing.

Read about Margaret Sanger, the racist founder of Planned Parenthood. Learn about Maggie's fondness for eugenics and

---

[29] Formerly known as kidnapping.

ask your tween, if you wanted to eliminate a certain race and straight-up genocide wasn't an option, how would you do it? Then Google map Planned Parenthood locations together and discuss in what localities they reside.[30] Ask your tween to consider how today's threateningly low population replacement rate would be affected had the sixty-plus million babies aborted since *Roe* had been allowed to live. Ask your kid how human behavior might change if "choice" was not an option.[31]

Seek out the pro-choice talking points and learn the easy ways to debunk them. Whether responding to "it's just a clump of cells," "my body my choice," or the more sophisticated "sure it's a human but is it a person?"[32] Stephanie Gray Connors is an excellent source for learning to make the pro-life case. Dig into the research on the lasting effects, both mental and physical, on women who've had abortions. Volunteer, even if it's just occasionally, at your local pregnancy resource center; advocacy for the unborn is best demonstrated when coupled with compassion for pregnant mothers.

. . .

---

[30] Spoiler alert: poor minority neighborhoods.

[31] Thought experiment: Say the "choice" to kill babies that result from consensual sex was not a thing. That would mean you would be pretty careful about whom you did the sex with. It would certainly be important to have the other party committed to you, since you both know if you get knocked up it's a lifetime gig. How do you know someone is committed in that way? Only marriage. An exclusive marital sexual relationship inhibits sexually transmitted infections, out-of-wedlock births, child poverty, and so much more. It's almost as if abortion made everything worse.

[32] One of the many topics addressed at CanaVox.com, teen edition.

On the matter of race. Look up the definition of racism in an old dictionary, then look up the definition on dictionary.com. Discuss what changed and why.

Critique the 1619 Project together and research dubious claims, using primary sources whenever possible. Then spend some time reading essays from 1776Unites.org and determine which narratives adhere more closely to historical truth.

Read *The Hate U Give* by Angie Thomas, then read Monique Duson's[33] book review and discuss whether your tween was able to see for themselves how the story is a gateway drug for racial indoctrination. If you're more the listening type, we've found the *All the Things* podcast by the folks over at the Center for Biblical Unity is a solid tool to aid in the development of a biblical worldview on race.

• • •

On economics. Become a consumer of biographies. Read the stories of those who have escaped socialist hellholes. Read[34] Marco Rubio's memoir, *An American Son*, and Ayn Rand's *Capitalism: The Unknown Ideal*. Study Cuba's decline into a one-party, communist-controlled state brought about by Fidel Castro's rise to power. Read reports of the shocking decline of living standards in Venezuela, once Latin America's richest nation.[35] Now 75 percent of the Venezuelan people live in poverty. Show your kids this terrifying example of socialist

---

[33] Center for Biblical Unity lady.
[34] Feeling overwhelmed at the voluminous recommended reading material? AUDIOBOOKS PEOPLE.
[35] In the 1950s Venezuela was the *fourth wealthiest nation on the planet*.

tyranny to illustrate how quickly socialism transforms a citizenry from night-clubbing until dawn to eating their dogs to avoid starvation.

The textbook definition of socialism is "government controlling the means of production." So politicians are lying when they claim that the high-functioning Nordic countries are "socialist." Debunk this lie by studying the capitalist societies of Denmark, Norway, and Sweden, which operate oppressively expensive social safety nets that require incredibly burdensome taxes to support. PragerU has so much excellent, age-appropriate content on many, if not all, of these subjects. Some videos even have handy quizzes afterwards to test the viewers' retention.

The World Is Still Your Classroom

We're mothers, known for nagging and repetition—thus, again, *you* are the program. The world provides so many opportunities for teaching, and, lucky for you, lesson planner, reality stands firmly on the side of conservatism. Whereas in the elementary years you use the world to teach what is true, middle school ushers in the more sophisticated, nuanced season of using the world to debunk lies and sussing out agendas.

- A news reporter uses the phrase "pregnant people" in a story supposedly about access to health care. Full stop. Ask your kids why it is that so many people under the Woke spell cannot define what a woman is,[36] yet *Roe v. Wade* is overturned and suddenly everyone knows exactly what a "woman" is? Take away: the Wokist worldview is incoherent because Woke ideas are based on feelings—not reality. When ever-changing feelings build a foundation, the structure will inevitably crumble.

- Your local park has become infested with hobos,[37] and the police cannot, or will not, do anything to clear them out. Do a drive-by and talk about how letting people live in squalor in the parks not only detracts from the beauty and usability of the park, it's unloving. It wasn't like this ten years ago; what changed? The idea that we should "decriminalize" homeless and "help" them through massive government spending[38] is what changed. Takeaway: when poor choices are rewarded, poor choices abound.

- Tune into news media and watch abortion advocates screeching about the "right to choose," talk about the true nature of choice, and how choice was actually exercised when the two participants chose to engage in sexy time. Emphasize that the only difference between those screeching activists and a baby in

---

[36] Newly minted Supreme Court Justice Ketanji Brown Jackson doesn't know what a woman is. Except she's celebrated as the first black woman to be confirmed for the court. Wait a second...

[37] Yes, hobo. Bum works too. Junkie thief, ne'er-do-well, and vagrant will also suffice.

[38] By some estimates, Seattle spends $100,000 for every homeless man, woman, and child. Nearly double the average individual income. https://www.city-journal.org/seattle-homelessness

the womb is time. And point out, as Ronald Reagan famously said, "I've noticed that everyone who is for abortion has already been born." Takeaway: on a human level, the only difference between a fetus and a pro-choice screecher is that one's right to life is protected and the other's right to life is under attack.

- News of the premature death of the four-hundred-plus-pound "fat-acceptance" Instagram influencer shows up in your newsfeed. Watch some "fat is beautiful" and "destigmatize obesity" videos together and discuss how reality is going to reality regardless of what we call it.

"Ideas have consequences. Bad ideas have victims." In one brilliant sentence, John Stonestreet[39] perfectly summarizes the theme of middle school training. Victims of Woke ideas are everywhere; spend the middle school years drawing real-world connections between Wokist ideas and the human suffering that always follows in their wake.

---

[39]   Colson Center president and all-around Christian conservative house afire.

Do not miss this critical window to help your tween learn to identify the myriad crooked sticks in their world because the time for *teaching* is drawing to a close. Your promotion to the role of consultant is nigh.

CHAPTER 8

HIGH SCHOOL—STAY CONNECTED

This chapter doesn't require ten pages on tactics for helping high schoolers. It could be distilled into a simple two-word sentence: stay connected. That's the only way to help your conservative teen navigate the perils of a Woke high school.

• • •

I, Katy, am a great deal better than my wrecking-ball coauthor at many things. One of those things is working, most especially work on any of our writing collaborations. This means that if I don't provide Stacy's pen knife with fresh meat, she will blissfully do nothing, zip, zero. Because of my greater gifting and exceptional work ethic, the duty to incept falls to my already burdened shoulders. Instinct tells me that our publisher would like more than a two-word chapter, no matter how much Stacy would relish such quick work. Thus I sat, staring blankly at the slightly ominous glowing screen of my MacBook, pondering the ways I could expound on "stay connected" to motivate Stacy's wrecking-ball ways, when I received the following text from my freshman son.[1]

"Yea, so I was shut down by Mrs. Anderson."

We suspected that friction between Josh and his history teacher was likely to develop. During the open house, Mrs. A had proudly proclaimed that sniffing out "misinformation" was to be the paramount focus of classwork during the first semester. The current assignment was a group project presenting information on both sides of a challenging topic, for which Josh's group had chosen abortion.

The following is the unedited exchange between my son and me, in all of its unpunctuated, uncapitalized, incomplete-sentence glory:

Mom: What happened?

Josh: so the people in my group were like saying why are we talking about abortion it's not a big deal girls can choose and i said it is a big deal millions of kids are murdered each year then mrs anderson saw that her precious kids were losing an argument and she came over and said like alright you are being rude and she said where are your sources and how do they come into play here and i said i have multiple sources from the credibility checklists you made us do do you want me to show them to you and she was like no that's not the point and she was like we need to be opening up conversation and i said i am i am debating them and she was like no you are being rude and i was like ok and then for the rest of the class i made a google doc on sources that will help me win an argument with her next time

---

[1] Stacy is entirely responsible for this paragraph. While she might be 100 percent correct, Katy would never write such a self-congratulatory statement, no matter how true it might be.

Mom: So she didn't like your tone, is that it? Was your tone different from the other kids or was it simply that you weren't affirming their opinions?

Josh: no i was questioning them. the only one de-incentivizing conversation was mrs anderson she claims to be unbiased but shuts down people trying to reason

Mom: Correct. She has not had to live in a world where her ideas are challenged, and she's certainly never been in a world where the authorities don't share her ideology. She's swimming in biased water and doesn't even know what the water is.

Josh: she's gargling that water

Mom: What did the other kids in your group think?

Josh: they were all smirking like ooh the teacher shut you down

The time for teaching our son has passed. The support we provide in this phase is knowing, loving, believing in, and supporting him; we are his best advocates, team members with whom he can immediately reach out after his blind-to-her-own-biases teacher turns a legitimate student contention into a public shaming. He feels connected enough to his dad and mom, so that when he finally gets to his advisory period and can safely pull out his phone, we are his go-to for consultation; we are the voices that tell him:

> "That's garbage. You were winning so she just put
> her finger on the scale and tipped it toward your
> pro-choice classmates. Stand tall. The battlefield
> is uneven but you are a champion for those who
> cannot beg for their own lives to be spared, you are
> a warrior."

Over the next few days, Josh transformed himself into an authority on the pro-life position; he turned his beliefs on the matter into facts. We helped him research the pro-life position, exclusively using sources that Mrs. Anderson had previously deemed credible, which resulted in the following text exchange:

Josh: i had some good debates with [Mrs. Anderson] where i got her to admit she was wrong

Mom: REALLLLLLY

Josh: and i made her stumble a few times

Mom: Good man.

Josh: she would stop talking for like 5 seconds and then nervous laughed whenever she was stumped

To the best of our ability, we saturated Josh in truth and beauty when he was young. We modeled conservative values throughout his elementary years. Introducing him to Woke ideas came earlier than we'd have liked because he heard his two older sisters asking questions about the crooked sticks they were encountering in middle school. We immersed him in Sunday school classes at church, and he'd participated in a number of study groups facilitated by CanaVox that explored matters of marriage, sexuality, and relationships from the natural law perspective. He knows the truth, and, more importantly, he's learned how to spot a lie.

· · ·

Once your kids' high school years commence, they are past the point of needing someone to tell them what's right and what's wrong. In fact, if you've got high schoolers in your orbit, you've likely observed that attempts to "teach" basic morality to your teens is about as productive as beating your head on the pavement. If, when addressing your sixteen-year-old, you utter the phrase, "Angel Baby, before you said that horrible thing to your sister, did you consider whether your words were useful, thoughtful, and kind?" it's a safe bet you've missed the *truth and beauty*[2] window that's only open for business during their elementary school years. Trying to pry that window open in high school will almost surely result in your teen tuning you out and pushing you away.

The Connected Consultant

The high schooler doesn't need a teacher. They need a consultant.[3] They need parents who encourage them to live out their convictions, develop their ideas, and apply those truths to real-life situations. At this age, you should already have helped your teen whittle their straight stick against which they can measure Woke claims, and in more nuanced situations, when they're unable to suss out exactly why their conservative straight stick isn't revealing the wrong-think they've

---

[2]   That's the last time. Katy's been cut off and threatened with sanctions if she cannot control herself going forward.

[3]   Modern American parenting is confused and backward. Parents function as consultants to their free-wheeling, "self-directing" toddlers, loath to impose discipline or consequences. Then they find themselves forced to micromanage out-of-control teens who never learned self-discipline or self-management as the consequences of their laissez-faire parenting approach. Good parenting is the inverse. Train your littles in self-control through enforced boundaries and then slowly loose the reins as you move into the role of teen consultant.

encountered, you're available to help them figure out how to better align their stick against the crooked world.

There are two equally important attributes the effective consultant must possess: expertise and accessibility. That's why it's paramount that *you* be the expert, as we covered in chapter 3. Your kid needs to know that you're a trustworthy source of solid information. However, the consultant's expertise is useless if they are not *available* to consult.

Think about it in terms of a fitness consultant. Say you were suddenly possessed by the idea that you should run away to join the Cirque du Soleil because you obviously missed your true calling and should, instead of writing, be traveling the world performing elite aerial arts.[4] Would you hire a fat-positive, fast-food-addicted fitness consultant who always let your call go to voicemail? Not if you wanted to realize your run-away-and-join-the-circus dreams. You would seek a fit aerial arts expert, a professional who would coach you in real time while you tried not to strangle yourself with the silks.

When dealing with the circus of public education you're not only the safety net beneath your kiddo, there to catch them when they inevitably fall, but also the consultant who is advising them on how and when to stay strong because the show must go on. A productive consultant-pupil collaboration necessitates not just expertise, but accessibility and connectedness as well.

Being the recipient of your kids' post-history-class-tussle text takes more than *knowing* you're on the same ideological

---

4   Stacy's family will miss her very much.

page; it means they know they can count on you to respond when they call. That means that you have to do whatever it takes to stay connected to your teen, a task that even rock star parents struggle with.

We all know, whether we're parenting teens or simply remember being one, the high school years are not famed for being a time of parental serenity and a strong parent-child connection for a variety of reasons, some of which are beyond a parent's control. Yet, the one thing you do have complete control over is your *accessibility*.

The biggest challenge to connectedness is often busyness—both yours and theirs. At this age, your kids are becoming more independent and are actively participating in meaningful activities outside the home. Between sports, part-time jobs, church, youth group, friends, crack-of-dawn jazz band, after-school clubs, and school itself, it's unusual to catch a glimpse of your teenagers, much less spend meaningful time with them. We caution you to not mistake their busyness and budding independence for a lack of need for emotional connection with you. They need you, as their consultant, their supporter, and most importantly their *parent*, during these years as much as they ever have. The high schooler's need is just more cerebral.

Staying connected is impossible without emotional closeness, and emotional bonds are impossible to knit absent physical closeness. Maintaining physical proximity is challenging with one busy teen; in a family lousy with multiple teens the challenge of staying physically close is exponential. As of last week, and for the next six months, the Faust home will house four teenagers. One is college-age, and the younger three are going in different directions all day, every day. Remaining connected requires prioritizing, scheduling, and creativity.

• • •

Prioritizing. In what's likely the final four years of sharing a roof with your progeny, the battle for your time and attention will be fierce. During this phase, you're finally tasting some real relief from the physical labor small kids require.[5] High schoolers should be managing their own schedules and packing their own lunches. Some might even be making you a cup of coffee in the morning.[6] Having older kids ushers in a season during which you have some time to pursue the interests or activities you set aside a decade ago.[7] This is a good thing, but your hobbies, self-assignments, or increased workload must not supersede the attention and time your kids need.

You demonstrate that they are your highest priority by leaving work early to cheer them on from the sidelines at the soccer field in the miserable rain. They know you're invested because when your teen, who *really* needs to talk, gets between you and your mattress at way-past-sleep o'clock, and instead of asking if it can wait, you resign yourself to making that 5:00 a.m. espresso a triple shot. You prioritize your teen when you take the time to help her write that gun-control essay in a way

---

[5]   Let's be real. It's a deathwatch for the first five years, first ten if they're boys.
[6]   If that's the case, we suggest keeping that tidbit to yourself, assuming you want to retain friends.
[7]   The chance that Katy could have started a nonprofit or Stacy could do all the crazy yoga she's into with kids under five years old is statistically zero.

that dances the line between her Woke teacher's expectations and her own conscience, even though your favorite team is playing on *Monday Night Football*. In this stage of parenting, you've been relieved of seat-belt-buckling duty, cleaning boogers off the couch, and yelling at them to brush and floss. Keep these newfound parental freedoms in mind and make a point to embrace the often inopportune moments when they *do* need your time and attention and make those moments priority number one.

There are some seasons when this is more challenging than others. For parents who work from home, summer is the absolute worst.[8] The workload doesn't change, but the time to accomplish it is under constant attack by "I know it's last minute, but I forgot to tell you I need a ride to wherever again" or "Mom! I need your help! I've looked *everywhere* but can't find the thing that turns out to be right in front of my face but apparently only you can see." Or our hands-down fave, "I TOLD YOU I needed this special thing that you can only get at this special place by tomorrow, the place is half an hour away but closes in twenty-five minutes, and can I drive?"

• • •

Katy here.

The following fiasco has been noted in my permanent record of parenting failures, in blood-red Sharpie I'm sure, as an Official

---

8   Whoever named that horrible break "vacation" is fired.

Reprimand.[9] You see, writing and deadlines make me a bit crabby, and time was running out to meet a deadline for an article I'd been assigned. Late that evening, after a day filled with one of the afore-mentioned time-sucking teenisms after another, my sweet son made the mistake of sitting down next to his crabby-pants mother and asking, "Mom, can we talk?" Crabby-pants barked, "NO. Leave me alone. I have to get this done. Please."[10] His response was to remain seated, unmoving, staring at me. Five minutes elapsed and he was still there, his father's soulful carbon-copied eyes boring into the back of my laptop. Lost in my big, stinky crabby-pants, blind to anything but my looming deadline, I brushed this behavior off as him mess-ing with me, another not-as-attractive trait he'd also inherited from his father, so, assuming he was playing games, I doubled down, "Seriously, Josh you have to go away! We can talk tomorrow." He went away. Tomorrow came and went without conversation, so did the next day, and the following. The days of very little talk piled up until his heartbreak was too much, and he couldn't carry his bur-den alone any longer; he showed me, through his tears, the depths of how much I'd left him hurting for a week. Crabby pants might be

---

[9] This is not actually a thing. There is no Official Parenting Record. However, you will have to answer to God for how you parent your kids, so, operating as if it is a thing? Not the worst idea.

[10] I'd added the "please" as an afterthought, by no means did I mean it.

uncomfortable, but the cone of shame?[11] *Avoid it at all costs, I earned and wholly deserved that Official Parental Reprimand.*

. . .

Work, meetings, the Broncos, and deadlines will still be there in four years; your high schooler will not. Prioritize their emotional needs above your other duties.

. . .

Scheduling. Living in modern society requires scheduling. Doctor appointments, meetings, your color and blowout, landscaping, manscaping, septic tank maintenance, veterinary visits. All of which fall below the level of importance of connecting with your high schooler. You might find yourself home with your teen on occasion, but you cannot count on such accidental circumstances regularly. Scheduling is required to guarantee time with them.

Maybe that means a weekly breakfast date at the iHop at crack-of-dawn o'clock, or maybe you establish a take-your-daughter-to-Barre-class Wednesday tradition and follow it up with guilty-pleasure onion rings because you've obviously *earned them.* A sit-down dinner together at least once a week is another important time for connection, even if that sit-down dinner is takeout pizza. Whatever your schedule, it's up to you to carve out time with them. No matter how demanding your

---

[11] This is a thing. Ask your dog.

calendar might be, it's more flexible than the visiting hours at juvenile hall.

• • •

Creativity. If you're like us, the demand for your time regularly outstrips your supply. To-do lists only seem to grow, and on the blue moon chance that you actually complete all the to-dos, in reality, it just means you've forgotten something, usually something important. Even if you are not tethered to a forty-hour work week, it's difficult to manage multiple kids and keep the home fires burning. But with a little creativity, maintaining a connection can be done. Travel for work? Take a kid with you. They can manage themselves in the hotel or visit a local museum during your meetings. Headed to the gym? Make a kid your workout buddy. Are they home due to the ever-multiplying "teacher planning days"? Make them your Costco date.

Another fantastic tool in your stay-connected parenting arsenal is the car. We all spend a stupid amount of time driving our kids to and fro, and sometimes it's easier to talk about something disturbing they saw on Instagram or share an embarrassing social fail with you when you're not making eye contact. Even better, add more teens to a car ride. It is one of the cheapest forms of entertainment. We can't recommend carpool duty as a time to connect highly enough. Matter of fact,[12] the car is the very best place to trap teens with whom

---

[12] Not fact, but informed by unscientific observation and feelings. Because we're women.

you're feeling distant; take the long way home, drive the speed limit, and forbid earbuds. By forcing connection in close quarters, it's possible to close the gap between you and your teen.

So-called quality time cannot be manufactured; quality time tends to emerge during quantity time. In this busy life, you will never "get around to" nourishing a relationship with your high schooler. Instead, choose to view their presence in your day-to-day goings-on as an asset instead of a chore. You help usher them into adulthood in a relational way.

It's going to take prioritizing, scheduling, and creativity to make sure that you remain in regular physical proximity to your teens. It is impossible to function as a trusted consultant if your teens feel like you don't know what's going on in their world because they never see you.

Principals of the Parent Consultant

If you've followed the process of the slow-handoff prescribed in chapter 5, your high-schoolers should be moving from Step 3 to 4. They are "doing" with your help, or you're kicking back watching them take on the Woke world on their own. Your job is more akin to a wingman now—you have their six—discerning which battles to pick and fortifying them to never compromise the truth.

Pick your battles. Your teens will need parental consultation navigating the perils of how and when to engage in battle. This is especially true if they are living in a Woke city where the opportunity for ideological battle can arise hourly, most especially if they are enrolled in public school. Fighting every battle is not, as the kids would say, *sustainable*. And choosing which battles are worth the fight will vary from kid to kid. Our girls, for example, are naturally more invested in relationships than are our boys; therefore they only whip out their conservative straight stick when they feel they must. Our boys? No matter the age, every last one is a hammer in search of nails, and they refuse to suffer Woke drivel from anyone. Therefore, in our experience, the boys have required more guidance in how to identify nails worth hammering.

Some situations will arise with peers, whether in their classroom or online, when kids are just not sure what to say or what not to say, even when they are equipped to make their case. Whatever the issue, the correct approach to hammering will depend on the day, the toughness of the nail, temperaments, and subject; and jointly discerning the best tactic. They need you, Mom and Dad, to be the adults with whom they consult when they can't discern whether to post or not to post, to be covert or overt, to let it go or let it all out.

Generally, there's no hard-and-fast dictate about when and how to engage. But there is a singular, concrete, one-size-fits-all culture war rule that every conservative, teen or adult, must adhere to. No matter the cost, never compromise on the truth. More straightforwardly? Don't lie.

· · ·

Don't lie. An understanding of the values you seek to conserve and the principles on which your family will not compromise will give clarity on which battles are worth the fight. That's why it's so important to spend their elementary years training your children in what they are *for* and studying the counter arguments in middle school. It's easier for kids to speak truthfully when they have a clearly defined belief system.

Beyond understanding what you are *for*, nonaggression is a good principle to live by and promote.[13] We tell our kids, you don't need to be aggressors, but you do need to stand firm. Don't pick fights, don't lob bombs casually, and don't unnecessarily provoke. But even a nonaggressor can get dragged into a fight; thus having a fallback defense is important. Tell kids of all ages that in those combative moments, especially if they are caught off guard, it's better to say nothing than to say something false.

In high school, they will be harassed by their teachers, pressured by their peers, and inundated with Woke ideology through library books, class materials, murals on the hallway walls, and Instagram reels. Sometimes Woke propaganda will sidle into your kids' orbit in the form of extended family members, even the nice ones who don't realize they've been trained to be clapping seals by CNN. These ubiquitous forces can wear on your teen, tempting them with the chance of a better grade or a momentary feeling of belonging if they pacify their peers by bending the truth. Living beset on all sides by the Woke can be exhausting, and it's human nature to yearn for acceptance, to be a part of the in-crowd, especially before our brains are fully formed. Talk to your children about the very real temptation to go along to get along and explain that lying is the short road to acceptance in popular crowd. Advise your teen that at

---

[13]   "Peace if possible. Truth at all costs." The original Martin Luther.

times, even when the desire to fit in is oppressive, it's better to remain silent than to prove yourself a liar.

Here is a mic-drop no-compromise anecdote from a high schooler neither of us can lay claim to—this young warrior's parents will be receiving the Raising Conservative Kids "Parents of the Year" award posthaste:

> A brilliant, bubbly, beloved and deeply committed young Christian friend of ours, while working quietly in class was confronted by her rainbow-flag-waving LGBT alphabet mafia– type table mate. Alphabet leveled her gaze at Bubbly, and, out of the blue, asked, "Do you think homosexuality is a sin?"

> As Bubbly recounted the exchange, she confided, "There was no way to be silent, and I knew I couldn't lie." Knowing the truth could cost her a great deal socially, she steeled herself and responded to Alphabet's challenge without compromise. She answered, "In the beginning, God made them male and female. Their bodies fit together like a lock and key. Two men can't fit together like that, and two women can't either. It's simply a matter of human design."

A+ little sister. She appealed to the goodness and indisputable complementary design of the body as an implicit review of same-sex sexual behavior; she didn't attack or get defensive.

This young woman knew what she was *for* and could defend her position without compromising.

Alphabet's response? "That makes sense."

Collision averted, this time. Bubbly knew quite well that the conversation could've gone the way of social suicide. Alphabet could've made a scene and proclaimed Bubbly to be a hateful bigot, turning the classroom mob against her. It took courage to speak the truth, but her parents had raised her to never compromise, and she'd learned her lessons well. Sometimes, however, *not compromising on truth can have social and academic consequences.*

• • •

Stacy here.

The Manning family is on a mission to rehabilitate the reputation of Christopher Columbus. So far, I wouldn't say our campaign has been popular with many of the Manning children's humanities teachers. Unfortunately for Evelyn, her English teacher was a rabid Columbus hater, who made a point of propagandizing her captive audience on the reg with the usual, "Columbus was a rapist and murderer" lie, obviously ignorant of the historical truth about this great man. As Columbus Day, rather Indigenous People's Day[14] approached, Columbus Hater assigned Evelyn's class a persuasive essay.

Evelyn saw an opportunity for some Columbus rehab work and got busy writing. Using Columbus's own words, from letters he himself had penned, she wrote a compelling, factual essay in the style

---

14   EYE ROLL.

of her usual grade-A work. For which she received a C. Righteously angry, she approached her teacher to inquire as to her undeservingly bad grade. The teacher's main issue with her paper (you just cannot make this stuff up) was that Evelyn had used primary sources. Hater's beef with Evelyn's work was that she had the audacity to analyze and think for herself instead of using some scholar's filter to gather information.

Evelyn learned some things in that class, but improving her writing ability was not among them. She learned about abuse of authority, and not to trust people in positions of power to name a few. She also learned that sometimes speaking the truth will result in punishment, and to do it anyway.

Evelyn also benefited from knowing she had available, expert consultants in her corner. She was pretty peeved[15] having suffered this injustice, but when she'd simmered down a bit and gained some perspective on how good it felt to not back down? Ms. Hater became the butt of many a Manning joke, at which we all laughed, because that teacher's nonsense was laughable. And laugh we did, because, connection.

---

[15]   Murderous.

CHAPTER 9

← — — — →

ATTACK IDEAS, NOT PEOPLE

*S*tacy here.

Reports of my cancellation have been exaggerated; however, the attempt to do so was personal and depressing.

I'm a cliché SUV-driving, yoga-teaching suburban mom. At the time of my attempted cancellation, I was also a gymnastics coach at a small business located in our quaint little downtown.

Pride month was upon us, and the mob was thirsty for a fresh conservative sacrifice. Unfortunately for me, a lesbian mom who practiced yoga at the studio where I taught, who also happened to have her kid enrolled in my gymnastic classes, discovered another side hustle of mine was working with *Them Before Us*. TBU is Katy's nonprofit organization on a mission to advance the scandalous idea that kids have a right to their mom and dad, but ignorant, hateful, crazy people with zero ability to think critically believe Them Before Us to be an anti-LGBT organization—a bogus charge entirely without standing. Without approaching me, or seemingly doing any investigating at all, this lesbian mother riled up a mob of Wokist[1] mommies who unleashed a smear campaign on this not-very-humble coauthor by way of an email barrage, demanding these two small businesses fire me. A friend of mine who had infiltrated this group, warned me of the coming swarm via screenshots of the hysterics masquerading as conversation on their hate-has-a-home-here mom's Facebook group page. The slanderous things these strangers were saying about me were shocking. Worse still? I knew some of these locusts, some merely on social media, others whose phone numbers were saved in my Contacts. The gory details of the affair are tedious and irrelevant to Raising Conservative Kids, but for the sake of closure, in the end, the mob was unsuccessful and I remained employed by both entities. However, the experience left me feeling defeated, wronged, and surrounded by haters.

Of the mothers who wanted to rob me of gainful employment, not one deigned to open a dialogue with me, not one made any effort to discover for themselves whether these baseless anti-LGBT charges had merit. Instead, they followed the widely favored leftist tactic of attacking me rather than attacking my ideas.

I cannot adequately describe the hate I have in my heart for this Wokist mob.[2] I would only save any one of them from drowning if I was sure they would perish from dehydration on the beach afterward.[3] Does my visceral hatred of them make me a good person? Nope. Am I proud of my inability to rise above? I'm not. But it's the truth.

---

[1]   Much like locusts, Wokist mobs mindlessly devour whatever is in their path, leaving only devastation in their wake.

[2]   That whole love your enemies direction Jesus gave His followers is the most annoying and difficult of all His directives in one author's mind. Bet you can guess which one.

[3]   TRUTH.

I've shared the story of my attempted cancellation because I know intimately what results from attacking people and not their ideas. These women[4] attacked me personally, and it engendered in me, a seemingly reasonable well-adjusted[5] Christian, durable loathing for them when previously there was none. What's more, will I ever entertain one counterpoint to my ideas that escapes any one of their ignorant, hate-filled pieholes? No. Attacking people only serves to reinforce your target's opposition to your ideas and makes you their undying enemy.

• • •

Responding with anger toward these misguided people and their stupid ideas is understandable; after all, the damaging public policy that flows downstream from them is obviously having a detrimental effect on our daily lives and putting our children's future in jeopardy. Whether their motivation to destroy America is malicious or, the more likely case, they're playing the part of useful idiot[6] easily manipulated by the Wokists, they *are* responsible for damaging our culture. However, to be an effective shaper of positive change in our sick culture, your anger must be directed at the bad ideas not the people who hold them.

---

4   HARPIES.

5   Mostly.

6   Not our phrase. The term "useful idiots" was used by Joseph Stalin to refer to innocent and/or well-intentioned sentimentalists or idealists who aided the Soviet agenda.

The deep social dysfunction afoot in our country is analogous to a dysfunctional family.[7] When communication between family members has deteriorated to the point that a therapist is consulted, the concept of escalation is one of the first dynamics they will explain. It's a simple principle; once someone raises their voice, the other party raises theirs in kind. Thus, opposing parties tend to escalate their conflict to the point of shouting at one another, which is likely the very reason they've sought family counseling in the first place.

It's human nature to match tone, so it goes against our instinct to keep shouting at someone who won't shout back. Training yourself and your children to remain calm during interactions that have the potential to escalate is a tactical way to defuse anger. Better still, learning to lower your voice makes it even more difficult for your opponent to escalate and reveals their irrationality if they do. Dulcet tones can compel the listener to simmer down, and maybe even lean in.

Steven Crowder, of *Louder with Crowder*, provides an excellent example of how to lower the volume in his "Change My Mind" series. You can view his G-rated segments on Rumble. com.[8] He sets up a table, usually on a college campus, with a sign that says something incendiary like, "There Are Only Two Genders—Change My Mind," or "Male Privilege Is a Myth—Change My Mind." Then he invites strangers to sit down and take their best shot at changing his mind. These are educational and entertaining videos and a great resource on how

---

[7]   Stacy is expert in identifying dysfunctional dynamics; she assures me this is a proper analogy.
[8]   Also YouTube, but don't support those commie bastards. Rumble doesn't censor. Can't say that for YouTube.

attacking ideas, not people, is done well. The most important takeaway from Crowder's approach is this: he knows that the vast majority of people willing to sit down with him will *never* change their minds, but he uses them as a foil to change the minds of those in the audience. He's aware that the audience members are the most likely to be persuaded by his Socratic approach to the conversation.

On your parental campus, your audience is your children, and they need to see you attacking ideas and not people. Thus, construct your arguments on these four guidelines:

1. Make them reason-based, not feelings-based.

> *"The first man to raise a fist is the man who's run out of ideas."*
>
> H. G. Wells, *Time After Time (1979)*

The Woke's vision of man exalts feelings above all. Carl Trueman, professor at Grove City College, refers to this idolatry of emotion as our era's default conception of self.[9] He describes this view of self not based on what has historically been a transcendent order[10] but rather "expressive individual-

---

[9]   If you're a smarty-pants with oodles of time on your hands, read Trueman's *The Rise and Triumph of the Modern Self*. If you're a mom who is barely keeping her head above water, read his simplified *Strange New World*.

[10]   In past eras, people would look to external structures such as their family, nation, or religious framework to answer the question "Who am I?" Now, those institutions are often considered oppressive; thus, only personal feeling remains as a guidepost for identity formation.

ism"; that is, the Woke's exaltation of preferences, eroticism, and emotivism as the ultimate good.

The problem with idolizing emotion is the same problem that has always resulted from idolatry. Idolizing the false god of feeling warps reality; thus feelings-based living is an untethered way to live your life. Due to the changing nature of emotions, when feelings subvert the facts, reality must bend to suit the feels. This ruled-by-passions mentality explains why some people can say "trans women are women" and genuinely believe it.

Ben Shapiro of The Daily Wire might be correct when he says, "Facts don't care about your feelings," but Tim Pool of Timcast strikes closer to today's Woke mindset when he says, "Feelings don't care about your facts."

It's easy to react with outrage to lunatic, feelings-based utterances like "a heartbeat at six weeks is a manufactured sound designed to convince people that men have the right to take control of a woman's body."[11] We understand the allure of letting emotions lead the way: it is effortless; requires no training, no discipline, no thinking; and is immediately emotionally satisfying. But if you're picking up what we've been laying down in this book, conservative training is a long-road journey. As conservatives we must cultivate and model for our children the ability to be governed by truth greater than our feelings.

The Woke's attack-people approach suits a feelings-based worldview: against the rightness of the right, it's all they've got because their worldview is incoherent, and incoherence is

---

[11] Ladies and gentlemen, the governor of Georgia, Stacey Abrams.

indefensible. When there's no rational argument to be made, a vitriolic personal attack is the only option, and the Wokists have an army of willing enforcers that come in the form of cancel culture, street violence, manufactured accusations of racism à la Jussie Smollett,[12] and mobs of rage-filled moms.

An attack-ideas approach best suits a reason-based worldview. It is coherent, and coherence is defensible. It's the rationality of our position that frees the conservative from resorting to personal attacks. Our worldview is girded by robust conversation, duked out in dialogue not the streets, confronts real acts of injustice, and rejects mob rule.

Employing the *method* of "attacking ideas, not people" is the compassionate, rational approach to changing hearts and minds and because right thinking is principled, this tactic reinforces the conservative *message*.

2. Employ robust rationale.

The progressives inhabiting Woke cities can spout self-refuting nonsense like "silence is violence" or demand to be called "they/them" because they've rarely experienced pushback against their nonsensical claims. Conversely, conservatives stuck behind enemy lines don't have the same

---

[12]   In the Woke world, demand for racism has outstripped supply. Thus, hate-crime hoaxes turn up every few weeks.

safety-in-numbers luxury[13]—every counter-cultural claim right-wingers make has the potential to cause the claimant some trouble, so you conservative types must model for your children how to withstand incoming scrutiny by using the attack-ideas-not-people approach, where reason is king and ad hominem attacks are beneath you. Expect you will not be extended the same courtesy, and if you are? Chalk it up to having met a unicorn.

When you push back against the progressive, feelings-based, detached-from-reality Woke worldview, you'll find it to be as fragile as the ego of many Wokists themselves. Like most forms of insecurity, ideological insecurity breeds aggressiveness in the form of personal attacks.

Unfortunately, attacking people, not ideas, has been a very effective leftist tactic deployed against those guilty of wrongthink. Whether threatening cancellation, lost employment, or your standing invitation to the swanky holiday party, fear of being the next sacrifice to the Woke god results in self-censoring and has had a chilling effect on the public discourse.

Because of the right's self-censorship, Wokist ideologues don't get the opposition to their ideas that they should. Thus, they are rarely, if ever, forced to defend or analyze their position. When anyone's ideas go unchallenged, people tend to become ideologically fat and happy, protected from alternative

---

[13]   Conservatives are like the training montage in *Rocky 4*: we're outside, dragging logs, running in the snow over rough terrain. In a Woke city, most people just assume you're a leftist and opportunities to disagree are countless. In other words, we know how to fight. Wokists are obviously Ivan Drago. Trying to shortcut their way to winning, big hat, no cattle style. Might look pretty, but when it's ring time? Rocky, baby.

viewpoints in their echo chambers.[14] As such, in circumstances where they *are* pushed to defend the indefensible and inevitably fail, they turn their sights on destroying *you* because they cannot destroy *your ideas*. As Ann Coulter has rightly observed, "If they call you a racist, you know you've won the argument."

Weak convictions and lazy reasoning are the outcropping of dishonestly contending with ideas, both of which spell destruction if the cultural deck is stacked against you. The importance of assembling an informed opinion cannot be understated, and that is exclusively the product of grappling with issues, not people.

For example, say someone holds an anti-gay marriage position because of the hedonism on display at the Pride Parade from the leather men, dykes on bikes, and drag queens. This extremely fragile perspective is founded upon disdain for a caricature, not by a depth of understanding of natural marriage and the social importance thereof. Thus, upon befriending a charming new gay coworker, who wouldn't be caught dead bare-assed in chaps,[15] they become pro-gay marriage.[16]

The same can be true if you're one of those right-wing types whose kids regularly witness you personally attacking your ideological opponents with insults like libtard dumbocrats.

---

[14] Smelling their own farts.

[15] Stacy wishes to be cremated floating-funeral-pyre style, set ablaze by her daughter via flaming arrow. She has instructed her children to dress her in chaps and her necklace made of their tooth fairy teeth.

[16] Several formerly staunch supporters of traditional marriage have changed their position after their own child came out of the closet, erroneously believing that distorting the definition of marriage is the means of loving their child. The proper response is to love your gay child AND defend the institution that best ensures that every child will have a mother and father to love them in the future.

Creative insults do not equip your kids for the culture war, but that kind of shallow opposition will make your kids into easy targets for the persuasive Wokist who appears to be thoughtful and charitable. Attacking ideas trains them in the *whys* of your belief system. The *whys* that undergird your *whats*, no matter how creative your name-calling skills, are the way to successfully persuade hearts and minds, and train your children to do the same.

This approach forces you to regularly contend with the actual arguments of your ideological opponents, and that will strengthen your worldview. Model for, and train, your children to do the same because they do not have the leftist luxury of cocooning themselves in a world[17] of safe spaces.

3. Use compelling tactics.

Understanding and calmly articulating the *whys* of your worldview will not win over everyone, but it will win some. Conversely, it's guaranteed that if you come out swinging with "listen, pukegressive," you will win few, and your victory will be a tarnished one. Real triumph, the kind of winning that produces long-term converts, develops in the wake of informed prowess, not verbal intimidation.

When you attack ideas you demonstrate to your opponent, onlookers, and especially your impressionable children that you're winning on the merits of your argument not

---

[17] The stories of conservative families spending a fortune to send their kids to college, just to have them returned as unrecognizable social justice warriors might not be a tale as old as time, but it's getting close. Don't let your child fall prey to the Woke cult by properly training them.

via intimidation, bluster, or empty emotivism. This is especially critical when you find yourself in the midst of a heated confrontation.

Mel Gibson,[18] director and producer of *The Passion*, chose the most beautiful music as the backdrop for the most horrific scenes of his film. During Jesus's crucifixion, the score reached a celestial apex. He juxtaposed beauty and brutality, torture so profound it was hard to watch, yet because of the captivating score, you couldn't look away. Be the beautiful music when you face off in a heated political battle in order to captivate the onlookers.

The reason we conservatives love watching video clips of Ben Shapiro "owning the libs" is because of his cool-as-a-seedless-cucumber demeanor. Another example of calm, pointed, and firm engagement can be seen watching Matt Walsh debate the topic of gender identity on *The Dr. Phil Show*. As the only dissenter countering a hostile panel and an unfriendly audience, Matt's pushback is a master class on attacking ideas not people. It's *almost* painful to watch the Woke panelists crumble at the slightest pushback. Almost. Round two of the Dr. Phil edition of attack-ideas-not-people comes courtesy of Lila Rose, who defends a child's right to life against a hostile audience and contrarian panelists.[19] In the face of aggression and high emotion, Lila calmly points to the facts and never escalates. Her beautiful disposition and tone stand in stark contrast to the angry, distorted face of the opposition. Lila knows

---

[18] His personal life may be a dumpster fire, but he does know what he's doing behind the camera.

[19] "Lila Rose Debates Abortion on Dr Phil: Fighting for the Right to Life for Children, Best Moments," YouTube, September 22, 2022.

she's right; she knows the facts, and her delivery validates her message.

The takeaway? Keep your cool. By modeling graciousness and rationality, your kids will watch and learn, and so will bystanders, whether online or at your neighborhood block party, and persuadable onlookers will immediately recognize which perspective has merit.

4. Show caring for the woke-ing wounded.

Refraining from attacking people is no small feat, especially when you're outnumbered in a Woke city. But beyond effectiveness, there's one more area where attacking ideas produces new fruit:[20] it may allow you to care for hurting people who have been swept away by the riptide of Woke ideas.

Those who live by Woke dictates are, not coincidentally, also often leading troubled lives. Self-described liberals, especially young, white, women, report drastically higher rates of depression and mental illness.[21] Destructive notions—such as abort your unwanted children,[22] casually divorce,[23] orient

---

[20] More Katy Christianese speak. Fruit is bible speak for developing admirable attributes in people.

[21] Why the Mental Health of Liberal Girls Sank First and Fastest, Jon Haidt, March 9 2023. https://jonathanhaidt.substack.com/p/mental-health-liberal-girls

[22] One study found that post-abortive women were 34 percent more likely to develop an anxiety disorder, 37 percent more likely to experience depression, 110 percent more likely to abuse alcohol, and 155 percent more likely to commit suicide. Priscilla K. Coleman, "Abortion and Mental Health: Quantitative Synthesis and Analysis of Research Published 1995–2009," Cambridge University Press online, January 2, 2018.

[23] Divorcees reported significantly higher levels of both depressive and anxiety symptoms. Gert Martin Hald, Ana Ciprić, Søren Sander, and Jenna Marie Strizzi, "Anxiety, Depression, and Associated Factors among Recently Divorced Individuals," *Journal of Mental Health* 31, no. 4 (August 2022), 462–470.

your identity around your feelings, sex-positivity, fat is beautiful, castigate friends and family[24] who fail to march lock-step with your Woke orthodoxy—may earn you Woke city street cred, but in the long term, these behaviors lead to meaninglessness, loneliness, and depression. And at some point, if the Woke spell is broken, those people will need help from the conservatives they've spent years deriding.

. . .

Katy here.

One of the more painful experiences of my life came from the difficulties between me and a close family member I'll call Bob for the sake of privacy. Bob took serious issue with my politics and my late teen conversion to Christianity. Our relationship became especially noxious once I began to assert my conservative beliefs through my non-profit work. As my message became more resonate and my reach greater, Bob's attacks escalated correspondingly.

Our every interaction, whether in person or online, involved him accusing me of being personally responsible for each degree of ocean temperature increase, for every foreign war, and for the death of any sexual minority he happened to see in his newsfeed. We had somewhat regular visits, and upon arrival I would insist that he and I immediately leave for a walk so my children would not see the vitriol and raised voice that had come to characterize the first half hour of our time together. I remember one don't-explode-in-front-of-my-children ambulation, Bob's fury was so over the top, our rage

---

[24]   Democrats are three times more likely than Republicans to unfriend on social media over political differences.

walk was replete with his spittle on my face. Bob was all in on the attack-people-not-ideas ethos, and because of it, he had burned out nearly every other non-leftist friendship he'd had, but because we were family,[25] *I became the acceptable target for all his wrath.*

This relationship devolved in a frog-in-boiling-pot manner, and it took me longer than it should have to erect better personal boundaries. When I finally did realize the water between us had heated to the boiling point, I laid down the law for further political conversations, none of which I initiated. My one rule was that Bob was required to discipline himself and focus his attack on ideas without attacking me. Miraculously, after he sought objective counsel, Bob actually changed his ways, and we had a mostly peaceable connection.

A year later, Bob was diagnosed with a devastating medical condition, and he was afraid.

I visited Bob in the hospital, and for the first time, we had a noncombative conversation about God. I read aloud and explained Psalm 23. I guided him through "letting requests be made known to God, so that the peace that surpasses all understanding could guard their heart and mind in Christ Jesus, our Lord." And then, astonishingly, we prayed together.

After what initially seemed to be a successful treatment, Bob died suddenly. Mine was one of the last conversations he'd had earth-side, a final conversation that never would have happened if I had matched his "attack people" tactics.

---

[25]   And my uncharacteristic willingness to be treated like garbage.

• • •

If you've reached the end of this chapter yet you remain unconvinced that our tactic is superior, perhaps the fact that attacking ideas instead of people makes you a better person will close the sale. Be the better person.

CHAPTER 10

↔

FIND YOUR PEOPLE

tacy here.

S When I first met Katy, I wanted to chuck her under the nearest bus. Bless her heart, she was a doe-eyed politically igno-rant neophyte. She was the wife of the new pastor just hired at the church where I'd been attending a Mothers of Preschoolers (MOPs) group; she burst onto the scene during an open gym for the preschool set at the local community center. Because I'm jaded and suspicious, I'm not one for small talk; I'm more inclined to conduct interviews of people who enter my orbit. Katy, vivacious and passionate, was managing my grilling well; that is, until we turned to politics and the needle slid right off the record. Much to my horror she breath-lessly described herself as a seeker of social justice.

Cue vomit in mouth.

Due to my unsaved, sinful ways, I decided to cause Katy and her freshly minted senior pastor husband an assload[1] of trouble by

---

[1] This word choice will make Katy squirm, but it's a biblical term. It refers to the measurement of eight bushels, taken from an annotated 1832 bible. Checkmate, unspayed female dogs.

tattling on her for being a leftist moron to the wife of a church elder. This wildly unchristian act is on the long list of sins I will eventually answer for. Nonetheless, at the time I knew that the last thing this stupid no-good leftist hellhole city needed was another social justice warrior (SJW), especially at the head of a church. It was an ugly affair, and the beginning of a beautiful friendship.

Recreational public shaming of my coauthor aside, I'm sharing this to illustrate that we've both had to do exactly what we're prescribing to you in this very book. She had some learnin' to do, just like the conservative education that I'd embarked on in my early twenties, when I realized that liberal didn't mean liberty. Fast-forward a decade and Katy's become a formidable, well-informed wing-woman.

During those MOPs years, park dates were peppered with plenty of political talk, well at least I talked a lot of politics, much to the dismay of some of the other moms, but some listened and engaged in conversation. Most were from the church where the MOPs group met and members of Jesus's fan club, so we, for the most part, shared a value system. I however, was the political junkie who knew more about politics than the bible. Some would have described themselves as liberal back then, but in our assessment, they were mostly an apolitical crowd, unwittingly drinking deeply of the tolerance/social justice Kool-Aid. Many political worldview shifts and clarification of right-thinking ways happened during those park dates. Some conversations were tense, some friendships waned, but for those that endured, the making of conservative moms meant the making of conservative kids. Moms and kids that my kids could trust and, more importantly, moms I could trust as right-minded counsel for my children.

These days you'll find this former bus-chucker sitting as far as possible from the one-time political neophyte as parent volunteer members on the first high school equity committee meeting. Our distance from one another a feeble attempt to conceal our right-wing tag-team intentions.[2] *We've become reliable sources of mutual support to one another, adults who fortify the other's children, and mothers to conservative kids our children can lean on. That's the power and value of "finding your people."*

Conservative Adults Need Other Conservative Adults

Living, and raising conservative kids, in a Woke city is a relentless exercise in resisting conformity. This is difficult because every human possesses a critical need to belong and is innately terrified of social rejection. This inherent, relational need is the tool the Woke have deftly wielded, asserting pressure to become "an ally" and "canceling" those who resist their extreme agenda. They have successfully forwarded their goals by leveraging the very tangible human fear of isolation.[3]

In 1951, psychologist Solomon Asch conducted a famous experiment that tested the impact of social pressure on conformity. He invited fifty male students from Swarthmore College to participate in a "vision test." The unwitting participants were brought into the lab, one by one, joining a previously assembled group of seven participants who'd been instructed to give

---

[2] Oddly, it's been a few months and the date for the next equity meeting is still TBD. Perhaps their claim that "perfectionism is an aspect of whiteness" and our response that this insinuates that students of color are less capable, made the district employees realize "reeducating" us might take more time than they were willing to commit.

[3] Read Stella Morabito's *The Weaponization of Loneliness* for an exploration of how historical and current tyrants control the population by manipulating our social impulses.

an incorrect answer when asked to identify which line, A, B or C, was the same length as the target line. Despite the glaringly obvious right answer, the seven ringers, as instructed, answered incorrectly. Asch discovered that, depending on the experiment's parameters, the unwitting participant conformed to the group's false answer 37–75 percent of the time, proving that the human yearning to belong is so strong that even during an inconsequential "vision test," with a negligible social cost, many men[4] were willing to go along with obvious falsehoods because the pressure to conform is inescapably powerful.[5]

Asch then repeated the experiment changing one variable, he added ONE other participant who gave the factual answer. The result? False answers dropped from 37 percent down to 5 percent. That means that having just *one* other person stand with you can buttress you to resist the mob and speak truth. That's why it is critical for you, conservative mom and dad, to find your people.

• • •

Stacy here.

---

[4]   We would bet all the monies, every cent of our vast fortunes, that if women were the subject of the study, the number conforming to the lie would be significantly higher.

[5]   Even though the wages of nonconformity can be high, keeping your dignity intact is priceless. During his freshman year, Rowan Manning learned that the national anthem would be replaced by the "black national anthem" ("Lift Every Voice and Sing") at the upcoming MLK assembly, and he decided in advance he'd remain seated if asked to stand; his convictions informed him that "The Star-Spangled Banner" was written for all US citizens, period, and that it was un-American to separate people by color. Rowan stuck to his guns, and he was the sole student in four hundred who remained seated. The social price he paid for this was high, but he learned who his real friends were and that doing the right thing is rarely the easy thing.

My awesome husband[6] made the mistake of running for city council the first time Trump ran for president. He was motivated to do so because our county executive, a Democrat darling, is using our small suburb as a dumping ground for all of Seattle's problems. Homeless shelters and state-funded drug dens intended to house and support the drug habits of addicted single males are two examples of bad ideas the county exec needed to have our (his) council members approve. So vital was the purchase of these Wokist council votes, that outside interests (predominantly union and Democrat Party money) contributed over $100,000 to the county-executive-preferred candidates.[7] That is a whole lotta dough considering our little city's population is a modest fifty-two thousand residents.

The campaign was the dirtiest local election anyone in these parts had ever seen. Trump derangement syndrome was of epidemic proportions, and the fierce vitriol toward my family was wicked. I was trashed and doxed on our most trafficked neighborhood Facebook[8] page, and my daughter was called a Nazi at school. The unfounded, vicious attacks my husband was subjected to, by our Wokist neighbors no less, were vile. The online threats were so out of control, that Mr. Manning directed me to avoid saying my last name in public.

There were a few people who came to our defense, those who knew that calling us white supremacists was insane, but not enough to give the rest of our crowd the courage to speak up. It was one of

---

6 Note to half of the voters in my hometown: THIS TOWN NEEDS AN ENEMA; YOU PROBABLY DO TOO.

7 Read: Woke SJWs and lawbreakers. Literally, my husband's opponent was a carpetbagging convicted criminal.

8 My Facebook flogging reigns as the longest thread on that page to date. People sure do like to kick us soul-stealing gingers around. Sleep with one eye open, haters.

the worst experiences my family has endured, and there was no jus-
tice, no happy ending.

    I share this story because the conservative adults in my circle
were the life rafts on this six-month sea of despair. They champi-
oned my husband and defended my family. They were a source of
encouragement and consolation, always at the ready to remind us
we were Right.

• • •

Safe harbors have sturdy docks, and sturdy docks require
many support piles driven deep into the sea bed for stability;
one pile would never suffice. In order to be a safe harbor for
your children, you will need to stand strong yourself, but one
pile does not make a strong dock. You need to stand with your
real-life people. No anti-vaxx Facebook page or school choice
Telegram group will suffice. You're going to need grounded
conservative friends. "But, where oh where might I find these
unicorns?" the kvetching reader cries out.

    Church.

    "But hypocrisy!" the kvetcher laments. "But I once had
a bad church experience!" the kvetcher kvetches. But but
but... Yes. We know. People have failed and wronged us too,
even the Christian types, and we've done the same, because
sin. Participation trophies for all. Now, enough with the wailing and gnashing of teeth. Take your family to, or back to,
church and join Team "I love the rockin' for Jesus worship!" or
the "Why can't we sing old hymns" crowd. Pick one; we don't
care which.

"The hubris!" the kvetcher bellyaches. "How dare you, not knowing where I live or what kind of churches are in my area, make such a blanket recommendation?" We dare because church, no matter how hard humans try to ruin it, is still God's Plan A for healthy spiritual growth and faithful community. Accept that the bible is a divine inspiration which accurately lays out the plan of salvation or choose to punch your ticket to hell; you can believe whatever you want. Even if you're not convinced that living in a whale's digestive tract for three days is survivable, you can't deny that Christianity is the basis for the founding of the most free, prosperous, and truly equitable society the world has ever known.

Not only is biblical living the recipe for human flourishing, it also prescribes the practice of moral self-examination from its fan club. Human beings are flawed, whether at church or Burning Man[9]. Better to surround your children with "Jesus is my Life Coach" types who are expected to acknowledge their flaws and work to overcome them.

There are, of course, churches that suck.[10] Churches that are allowing culture to disciple them, rather than discipling the culture. Whatever you do, stay away from sucky churches. Find a church that fought to keep its doors open during COVID, or the one with negative Yelp reviews because they wouldn't host a same-sex wedding, or the one with a male pastor. A good way to vet a church is by watching a few of their

---

[9] Burning Crotch Man would be a better description of that hedonist hole-and-a-heartbeat sex-fest. Two thumbs down.

[10] You know who you are, you vipers.

online sermons to ensure the bible is their authority. If so, the folks sitting in those pews have solid potential to be Your People. You might even find the kind of people who fear God so much that fear of the state or the woke mob pales in comparison. Our kind of people, your kind of people.[11]

Conservative Kids Need Other Conservative Adults

We have conservative friends from all walks of life. Some are involved in the grassroots fight against vaccine mandates. Some, outside of Mr. Manning, have run and are currently running for elected office. We know many who have become teachers, subversively providing a safe harbor for public schoolers. Some of our friends have recently discovered[12] their Second Amendment rights and are learning, and training their children, how to exercise their rights responsibly. We know entrepreneurs who bravely rejected government mandates to shut down.

These many friends of ours are not adult-exclusive relationships; they are friends to our children as well. Conservatism is not effectively taught as an abstract exercise, so it's important for kids to watch conservative values lived out in a variety of ways by a wide array of different adults.

. . .

---

[11] And if you're a Godless heathen like Stacy was fifteen-ish years back, the bonus of finding a church could be that these newfound people of yours might actually help God save your wretched soul.

[12] Who are we kidding, most of our friends are right-wing concealed-carry nuts with lots and lots and lots of firearms. Like, all the firearms. Utter the word "clip" around these folks? I wouldn't. But those who would make such a rookie blunder are now packing heat.

Katy here.

Because I'm the Uptight Pastor's Wife I'll use a church-y example. The old youth ministry model was a one to five adult to child ratio. The rationale was that if one adult poured into five different kids, every kid was "covered." A look at the decline in churched youth will tell you that is a failed model. One adult shepherding five kids does not a lifelong faith build. In reality, if your intention is to help a child build a rock-solid faith, or a conservative worldview, you need to invert the adult-child ratio. Every child needs at least five different trustworthy adults in their life with whom they can game out their choices, speak honestly about their struggles, and rest assured that those adults have their best interests at heart.

• • •

If you're winning at this parenting gig, Mom and Dad take the top two spots. That leaves three vacancies. If you are blessed, you have ample options among grandparents, aunts, and uncles. If you're lacking in the family department, or your family options lack merit, it's going to take some work. The other three spots should be filled with adults who share your values religiously and politically. The goal is to establish a tribe who can capably serve as trusted stand-ins for you, no matter the situation.

Incorporate your kids into your adult tribe by including them in these important relationships. Let them witness you vulnerably pouring your heart out to a trusted friend. Keep the door open when you seek her advice so your trust in her is transferred to your child by osmosis. Relationship modeling and friend selection is another aspect of the "I do, you watch" slow-handoff approach to training. When your kids have "watched" the trust you have established among your friend group, they'll know who to seek out when wise counsel is required. Optimally, parents will create a superstructure of trustworthy adults, and if you can start when your kids are young, all the better.

Conservative Kids Need Other Conservative Kids

Katy here.

In his freshman English class, my son Josh was assigned a blatantly biased prompt from which he was expected to write a persuasive essay about the theme of a short story they'd read. He pushed back, "I don't agree with your premise. This isn't just a story about racism; this is also the story of the triumph of capitalism." While the essay's subject family did encounter (in the mid-1980s mind you) mild discrimination, through pure grit and determination they successfully provided a life for their children that would have been impossible to achieve in the land from which they had fled. Chalking up a small victory for a high school freshman, his teacher relented and agreed to allow him to write his paper from his conservative perspective.

An out and proud Socialist classmate nearby smelled blood in the water, and in the standard-issue know-it-all SJW drawl, he quipped, "Akshually, capitalism is responsible for most of the inequality we see in the world." I'm sure he'd have dropped a mic had he been holding one.

"I don't think so," my son rebutted. *"I think global poverty has been seriously reduced since my mom was a kid, and it's because of the free market, not because of socialism."*

The insufferable socialist classmate, unaccustomed to debate, bristled, *"Oh really. Then why is it that these days CEOs make exponentially more than their factory workers than they did when your mom was a kid? Why is it that we've seen such a huge increase in the wealth gap?"*

My son realized he was well out over his skis and knew he was rapidly approaching the limit of his knowledge base. Further defense of his position would require Google or coming home to discuss the debate with his parents. Luckily, he was literally saved by the bell as their third period ended. The Socialist, still wanting his piece of flesh, inquired, *"Hey, where do you eat lunch? Let's debate."*

"In Mr. Carney's class, you should come," replied my relieved son because he knew what the Socialist did not. You see, my son doesn't eat alone with Mr. Carney; his lunchmates happen to be two of his conservative buddies, his peer Casey, and Stacy's eldest son, Rowan.

His retelling of the lunchtime sparring match during the car ride home sounded something like this:

> *"Mom, the socialist kid walked into Mr. Carney's class and just started in—bringing up people and events that I didn't know anything about. But Rowan? He had a response to everything this kid threw at him. The Socialist would make a point you could just tell he thought was a zinger, but Rowan would smack it down using a historical rebuttal, or he'd poke holes in his logic over and*

over. So then? The Socialist called in reinforce-
ments; other kids came in from the hallway argu-
ing against the free market. But Rowan took on all
of them just leaning back in his chair, coolly dis-
mantling their arguments point by point. Mom, it
was amazing. How did he know all of that? I want
to be able to do that."

Just like conservative adults need other conservative adults to wage battle online or attend school equity meetings in force, conservative kids need other conservative kids to provide reinforcement when they are outgunned. Further, Rowan did something for Joshua that only a peer could do; he modeled how it is possible for someone his age to calmly command a heated conversation, even when outnumbered.

That verbal lunchtime fisticuffs left a permanent mark on Josh. Like a lot of kids, he fritters away too much time watching anime and hilarious but unproductive Instagram reels. But these days, he is much more interested in gathering information. He's been asking questions about interest rates, European politics, and the legitimacy of FBI raids because conservative podcasts now consume more of his time than anime. Not because his mom directed him to, but because another conservative kid, a kid who graduates next year and thus won't be around to provide backup, showed him the value of filling his mind with logical and historical facts.

Neither of our kids has always, in fact I would say they have rarely, had friends at their public schools who could or would stand with them. But what they've always had is friends at their church who don't think that they are racist for failing to post a black square on Instagram, or transphobic for not stating their pronouns. They've always had a group of church peers whose full faces were gloriously on display during the pandemic and with whom they could appropriately mock the masks with holes for band class. Quite simply, they've always had friends who have also rejected the Woke, and it has helped them to stand firm, knowing they have a social refuge.

It's important for you to find these kids, the earlier the better, so they have at least one if not a dozen friends who can stand with them, fortify their convictions, and quite simply, affirm that they aren't crazy.

Seek the Conservative Light in Your Woke City (Hint: Look to the Hills)

> *"You are the light of the world. A city set on a hill cannot be hidden."*
>
> —Jesus Christ[13]

Boomers, and maybe even Gen Xers, are likely familiar with Ronald Reagan's description of American exceptionalism as a "shining city on a hill." The phrasing was his, but the concept was not. It comes from Jesus's Sermon on the Mount, and Reagan used Jesus's evocative imagery to paint the United States as a beacon of hope to the world. Reagan shrewdly used this uplifting allusion to inspire our nation to live up to its ideals by following God's righteous principles.

---

[13] SUPERSTAR.

But the city to which Jesus referred was not geographic in nature; it was spiritual. It's not composed of citizens inhabiting a physical nation, but populated by a heavenly people. It is not delineated by civic borders, it is an ethereal nation with enclaves worldwide.

Several years ago Mr. Faust spoke on this verse from the pulpit. He explained that Jesus was describing the existence of a distinct community within the city proper to which the Christians of Seattle, or Chicago, or DC, or Austin belong. In this quarter the people are governed by higher laws. Its community speaks using words that build up rather than tear down. Its people eschew licentiousness, and they rescue, instead of victimize, children. They share rather than hoard, favor stewardship over exploitation, and they are faithful among the faithless.

Your physical city may be governed by terrible ideas, but there is a spiritual light within your Woke city that abides by a distinctly different government and social order. It does not exist primarily to advance conservative ideas; however, it provides the best worldview framework within which conservative ideas can be lived out. Take refuge in the light of that spiritual city and find your people.

CONCLUSION

The turn of the eighteenth century found young Susanna Wesley, an impoverished British mother of ten, largely parenting on her own. By all accounts her husband was the obstinate pastor[1] type. When he wasn't preaching, he was obsessed with writing a commentary on Job that was universally considered unreadable. His pursuit squandered the family's resources and kept him largely absent from daily life. What Susanna lacked in husband-selecting ability, she made up for in the child-training department because she knew the importance of education, virtue, and orthodoxy—which she expertly replicated in all her children.

Susanna was serious about training from the moment her children were ready. When they began to speak, she taught them to pray.[2] Despite their grinding poverty, she taught economic reality to her children by "preserving property rights, even in the smallest matters." We assume the "smallest matters" meant she didn't take property disputes between her children lightly. Rather than outsource the honing of her

---

[1]   Unlike Mr. Faust, obvi. Katy's got the obstinance market cornered in that marriage. God help him.

[2]   Susanna was based. She taught them "to cry softly so as not to disturb others."

children's straight sticks to, as she saw it, a rigid, hierarchical, impersonal church system, she took it upon herself to provide each of them, her daughters included,[3] a world-class biblical and classical education.[4] Susanna was *the program* for training her kids.

In addition to hosting communal worship in her home and teaching her family biblical lessons, Susanna kept a regular weekly schedule[5] during which she invested an hour of one-on-one time with each child in order to stay connected.[6] Had she been our peer, we think she would have killed it on the Insta with her Rules for Raising Godly Children, in which it appears she was a practitioner of a hybrid version of the *no-flinch* and *don't lie* parenting strategies. She soundly advises, "To prevent lying, punish no fault which is first confessed and repented of." She was downright gangster.

Susanna quietly did the work necessary to replicate her belief system in her children, and in doing so she helped set the course for the Western world; yet, we'd wager you've never

---

[3] "That no girl be taught to work till she can read very well; and then that she be kept to her work with the same application, and for the same time, that she was held to in reading. This rule also is much to be observed; for the putting of children to learn sewing before they can read perfectly, is the very reason why so few women can read fit to be heard, and never to be well understood." https://faithgateway.com/blogs/christian-books/praying-example-susanna-wesley

[4] She also scheduled two hours of "alone" time in prayer. There was no coffee shop refuge, so she would pull her apron over her head and read scripture at the dining room table. Every kid knew to never interrupt.

[5] Susanna made spreadsheets before there were spreadsheets.

[6] Ten. Kids.

heard of her. Though, perhaps if you paid attention in US history class[7] you've heard of her son, John.[8]

John Wesley played an important, influential role in the Great Awakening. This religious revival is credited with a renewal of Jesus's fan club that helped to detach Christianity from the old-world pomp and circumstance religiosity of the crown. The Great Awakening in England but, more impactfully, in the New World resulted in a more cohesively knit Christian worldview among the colonialists. John lit a vision-shifting fire under the feet of the colonists that inspired them to embrace a new concept of nationhood. The Great Awakening perfumed the spirit of the American Revolution and its emphasis on spiritual autonomy helped train the eyes of the colonists toward a more democratic view of both church and state. The overarching concept of the Great Awakening was that of greater equality, which paved the way for US independence and the Constitution.

If you're parenting in America today, it's easy to fall into a "I can't make a difference" despair, believing all is lost unless you launch a successful podcast, get elected to office, or become a bestselling author. A demoralized opponent is the easiest to defeat so don't hand the Woke a victory by succumbing to hopelessness. Besides, it's just not true; quite the opposite is, in fact. Individuals have a powerful impact on the world, and you have a powerful impact on the children under your roof, kids

---

[7] We've both become so suspicious of everything, who can say whether it was ever trustworthy. But at least in our day it wasn't a constant stream of hate-on-America.

[8] And if you've found your church people, Susanna's son Charles has been aiding your worship via "Hark! The Herald Angels Sing," "Christ the Lord Is Risen Today," and "O for a Thousand Tongues to Sing."

who can have a powerful impact on their friends, their school-mates, and eventually the nation.

You may not have legislative or institutional control, or be able to insist that the classics be taught in your child's litera-ture class; but fear not, Mom and Dad: you have control over a mighty entity that has the power to stop the Woke agenda at your front door. Your family. It may be the smallest of insti-tutions, but it is the most crucial when it comes to replicating values. The potency of parental influence is the reason for the Wokists all-out campaign to supplant your role. The greatest nation-driving force isn't political power; it's parenting.

Susanna proved it. She was never elected to office, she held no degrees, and her influence was limited to her small town. But she was an informed, passionate Christian mother who replicated herself in her children[9] who, in turn, helped shape the Western world. John cemented his place as the most spar-kly jewel to adorn Susanna's mothering crown as she *watched* him *do* the world-changing work she'd modeled for him. Had there been no Susanna Wesley, there would have been no John Wesley. Without John Wesley the Great Awakening may not have occurred. Had there been no Great Awakening, it's possi-ble there'd have been no American Revolution.

Susanna is evidence that if you train your children well, your sons and daughters can similarly help revive Western civ-ilization. If it is true that history repeats itself, there's no rule that states such repetitions be limited to atrocities.

---

[9]   Ever hear of Methodism? It became the largest US denomination by combining "methodical," in-home, personal, and communal worship. John and Charles Wesley started it because they saw their mother live it. Unfortunately, today US Methodists are largely Woke. The Wesleys must be turning in their graves.

Short-Term Pain, Long-Term Gain

In the short term, the nation's future looks bleak. But there's reason to believe that we could be in a very different place in a few decades. The numbers are not known to be liars, and they tell us that the Woke are far less likely to form families.[10] They're either preventing conception to appease their Climate Change god, or they're drunk on the god-of-self Kool-Aid and are aborting the children they do conceive.[11] If they've not fallen prey to the aforementioned, some Woke parents have been convinced by the trans-cultists that the children they didn't abort were assigned the wrong gender at birth and would be better off chemically castrated. Furthermore, the progressive sex-on-demand culture has caused a meteoric rise in fertility-inhibiting sexually transmitted infections, and the alphabet mafia, by its very nature, results in the formation of non-procreative relationships. The data doesn't lie; Woke ideas are neither life-giving nor life-making.

This means that while the Woke might currently hold the cultural power, they are not producing children at a sustainable replacement rate; so, if we conservatives can successfully prevent them from infecting the minds of *our* children, this nation could look very different in short order. To affect the changes necessary[12] to revitalize this country, we need to out-number[13] and out-train the Wokists.

---

10 Either conservatives are more likely to marry and have children or marrying and having children makes you more conservative. Or both.

11 Making the proper sacrifice to Baal.

12 Be the change you want to see in the world already.

13 One dear friend of ours has so many kids they had to buy the church van; it seats twelve.

If you've decided to join us on this long road, trending news such as Richard "Rachael" Levine, the first "female" four-star admiral has been awarded *USA Today's* Woman of the Year, or political events like the Supreme Court finding hidden constitutional support for polygamy[14] will demoralize you. You might have a "Woe is us; all is lost. We've passed the point of no return" moment. We get it, we've had them too, but make your pity party short. Set a limit of one beer to cry into, and when you've seasoned your heady adult beverage with your salty right-wing tears, collect yourself and double down on conservative training. We need your company on this journey.

If you've decided to join us on this long road, you may also, on occasion, wrap up an episode of *Relatable* with Allie Beth Stuckey, finish reading *Live Not by Lies* by Rod Dreher, or shout at an empty house, "YES! WHAT HE SAID!" upon hearing Rep. Matt Gaetz's scorching committee grilling. You may be tempted to relax a bit, thinking, *Those people will save this nation.* Unlike you, they have massive platforms, write so soul-stirringly, and wield legislative power. While it is true that we could never have too many conservatives championing the cause in all forms of media, fine arts, and elected offices, they cannot be solely relied upon to save this country.

It is ordinary moms and dads, like you, like us, who will turn the national tide. Even if all our wildest dreams come true and The Daily Wire replaces CNN on airport TV screens, Republicans retake all branches of government, and American corporations return critical manufacturing from China to our

---

14 Any day now...

shores, those cultural, political, or industrial shifts are worthless if the next generation comes of age fueled by Woke lies.

So, the heavy lifting falls to you, conservative parent. It's going to be drudgery, a slog, and we may not see victory in our lifetimes, but it's possible that our kids will get to taste the fruits of our efforts. We said it in the intro but it bears repeating. You are not here by accident, neither are your kids. God put you and your children on earth at this time, in this place, for a reason. Go forth and train your children[15] not to be *transformed by culture*, but to be *transformers of culture*. You will not only save your kids from Woke destruction; you may save the nation from it as well.

What Say the Kids?

All right, we've exhausted our prattle-allotment[16] for the year; thus, we decided to turn the rest of this wrap-up over to our children. We asked them,[17] "What advice would you give to parents who want to raise conservative kids living in a Woke city?" We hope their answers will be an encouragement to you, but mostly our motives were selfish. The truth is that we were just fishing for more material to submit to the Parent of the Year selection committee and thought we could get some real mileage out of using our children's own words. Here's how they responded:

---

[15] "Go forth and multiply" was not a suggestion; it was direction. Do what you're told, people. Besides, sex is fun. Kids are fun. Be fun.

[16] Blathering is our spiritual gift.

[17] Note: save for getting their permission to share the stories in which they're featured, our kids haven't read this book. YET.

Ben Faust, 7th Grade—In Seattle, people try to twist the truth. But you and dad taught me how to detect lies. Dad helped me understand how Black Lives Matter wasn't really about racism, it was about a lot of other crazy things they were trying to teach and then they'd call you a racist if you disagree. You taught me that it's impossible to be transgender. Parents have to teach their kids to know right from wrong. And when their kids come home from school after hearing something crazy they need to be able to talk to you about it.

Josh Faust, 9th Grade—Okay. If you're growing up in a Woke city the main thing is you have to be an expert on everything, literally everything. Every topic. So parents have to become the smartest person their kid knows so he comes to you when he is told off.[18] Then you can give your kid an answer, but beyond that, you have to help them find good sources for future conversations. Also, if you guys were jerks, I'd be like, "man I'm going to reject everything you're saying out of sheer spite." So, since you guys are kind[19] (well, dad's kind anyway[20]) that's a big part of it. I wouldn't come to you if you didn't have a good relationship

---

[18]   Obviously still recovering from the sting of his chapter 8 history teacher scuffle.

[19]   "You gotta be strict, so they respect you. But not too strict, ya know?"

[20]   Spanking incoming.

with me, you know? So like, hang out with them, and find a show that you both like to watch—like a father/son show.[21] It's also important for kids to have good conservative friends. It sucks when the whole class is against you so it's great if you have someone to stand with you. And for the kid who has to stand alone my advice is—pray. Then summon your strength and speak the truth before you talk yourself out of it.

Miriam Faust, 11th Grade—The hardest part about living in Seattle is if you aren't careful, the world can start changing you, rather than you impacting the world. So parents really need to give their kids three things. 1. Quality Time. The more quality time you spend with your kids, the more likely they are to open up to you. And that's critical because if they don't open up to you, they'll open up to someone else. So be the one they turn to. 2. An Outlet. You need to provide them with a non-Woke outlet—where there are people, like wise older people they can talk to, who will be there for them. So basically, church or youth group. They need that weekly reminder of what they should stand firm in. 3. Daily Bible. First read the bible with them to help them understand

---

[21] 2022 was the year Ryan introduced Josh to *Magnum PI.*

what they're reading. That will create good habits that they can continue on their own when they're in high school. Encourage them to read in the morning, not at night, so they are reminded of the truth before they go out into the world.

McKayla Faust, College Sophomore—The worst thing you can do is shelter your kids. I can say that I'm now glad I grew up in a Woke city because I can see the effect of extreme sheltering on some of my classmates in college. They don't know how to defend their beliefs to those who disagree, because they were never challenged.

All that said, growing up in Seattle *was* hard. Parents need to understand the social cost their kids will face. A lot of people really hated me for my beliefs and attacked me personally. So while you can't shelter them, you also can't expose your kids too soon, otherwise they will become just like the culture. You need to make sure that your kids have a solid foundation before they are sent out into a progressive world.

You also need to know what's going on in their personal life so they don't act one way around you and another way around their friends.

So ask them good questions. Be patient and understanding during times that are hard. You have to develop a strong relationship. My dad especially was very intentional about taking me on daddy/daughter dates and retreats, taking me out for coffee and doing art with me. Also, if parents show that they know what they believe and why they believe it, it's more likely the kids will come to them with questions.

Miles Manning, 4th Grade—The best thing parents can do is teach their children the *right*[22] things.

Evelyn Manning 10th Grade—As a kid raised via this parenting method, there are three things that impacted me the most. The whole "stay connected" thing? That is no lie. My parents have really worked hard to stay close to me. With every teacher that has been against me, every classmate who's made underhanded comments, every "so-called" friend that walked away from our friendship, I knew I was always coming home to parents that would be there for me. Knowing this gave me the courage to burn a few bridges while spreading truth in the world.

---

[22] More profundity than he likely realizes.

Another very important aspect was being immersed in information while I was growing up. This gave me the ability to be confident that I knew exactly what I was talking about. Every second of my childhood was soundtracked by talk radio, and our dinner table conversations covered all things political and cultural, which helped to equip me for real world conversations. Hearing the facts over and over (my father's lectures are epic) made it easy for me to recall the facts when I needed them.

Finally, and maybe most importantly, my parents have taught me that it's OK to stand out. Whether by having weird traditions (like watching the *Fast and the Furious* series every December—yes, some of our Christian friends are super judgey about that), the examples they've been of never backing down when they're right, and the assurance they provided when I was unsure. I know that sounds cliché, but my parents have taught me that it's OK to be different. Trust me, being conservative doesn't go hand in hand with wanting to fit in. If my parents hadn't made sure I knew that it was okay to stand out, to be different, my mental state would be similar to the kids you see on TikTok.

Rowan Manning, 12th Grade—The best thing my parents, but mostly my father, did was that they taught me from as young as I can remember about the big picture and the morality behind economics, specifically the evils of communism and the blessings[23] of capitalism. My mom and I may have listened to hours of Rush Limbaugh, and she does make excellent sandwiches, but my dad explained the world clearly and made concepts easy to understand. My father really does know everything about everything, especially history. So, when I started to have my own experiences in the world, where I'd think, "something's not right here," I already knew what time it was.[24]

Well, it appears we will both be submitting nominations for that Parent of the Year award on behalf of our husbands.[25]

High on the list of our favorite Chinese proverbs is this: The best time to plant a tree was twenty years ago. The second best time is today. The conservative long road could use the shade, so get planting.

---

23 Rowan doesn't think this is the right word, but he was otherwise occupied explaining energy transfer to his brother while baking a pineapple upside-down cake and couldn't spare the time to find a replacement.
24 Inside baseball conservative talk for understanding the distinct perils of our time.
25 It would seem that we both did a bit better selecting husbands than Susanna.

ACKNOWLEDGMENTS

To our Misters. Thank you for doing the major bread-winning for our families; it is your steadfastness that provides us the luxury of chasing creative endeavors. Furthermore, without you two walking this long road with us, we'd not have the kind of kids that inspired us to write such a book.

Thank you to our children for becoming people that make us willing to risk writing this book before you've come of age.

And finally, thanks to the Wokists. We credit your diabolical ideas and downright insanity for forcing us to up our parenting game and for motivating us to inspire other parents to do the same.

ABOUT THE AUTHORS

Stacy Manning, senior editor for Them Before Us, is a standard issue, stay-at-home suburban mom, author, and side-hustle professional. It's also widely accepted that Mrs. Manning is responsible for inventing the raised middle finger, a.k.a. the Bird of Freedom. She and her husband of twenty-something years are raising their three children behind enemy lines in a suburb just outside of Seattle. When she's not sticking her meddling fingers in another writer's work, she is barefoot in the kitchen making her husband a sammich.

Formerly the picture of a peacemaking pastor's wife, **Katy Faust** is founder and president of Them Before Us, a global children's rights non-profit. Between soccer carpool and church duties, she's a mom on a mission against the progressive overreach—a globe-trotting speaker, hand-shaking policy influencer, and regular contributor to a variety of conservative outlets. Katy testifies and publishes widely on controversial topics such as "men and women are different" and "children should not be bought and sold." She helped design the teen edition of the Witherspoon Institute's CanaVox, which studies sex, gender, marriage, and relationships from a natural law perspective.